Hopeful

**A STORY OF AFRICAN CHILDHOOD
DREAMS AND THE RELENTLESS LOVE AND
SACRIFICE OF POOR PARENTS TO GIVE
THEIR CHILDREN AN EDUCATION.**

One poor family, started an education revolution that
challenged and changed perceptions, cultures.

ASA AHIMBISIBWE, MD

 FriesenPress

Suite 300 - 990 Fort St
Victoria, BC, V8V 3K2
Canada

www.friesenpress.com

ISBN
978-1-5255-4411-8 (Hardcover)
978-1-5255-4412-5 (Paperback)
978-1-5255-4413-2 (eBook)

1. BIOGRAPHY & AUTOBIOGRAPHY, PERSONAL MEMOIRS

Distributed to the trade by The Ingram Book Company

"Asa takes us on a remarkable journey that should leave us all hopeful."

—Tim Crothers, author of *The Queen of Katwe*

"Ahimbisibwe does vividly depict rural Uganda in a way that will intrigue audiences that may be unfamiliar with it, and he does so without exaggerating his characters' deprivations... Although the book carries a strong message regarding women's rights, it's not overly didactic, and it delivers an engaging story of how friends can maintain a connection despite life's challenges...An often compelling novel of poverty, hardship, and the promise of education".

—*Kirkus Reviews*

To all the women with a similar story: You are beautiful, and you make the world a better place.

And to my mother, for the relentless love, courage and sacrifice to give me an education. Rest well.

Prologue

"WILL YOU TAKE CARE OF MY COWS?" THAT WAS A MOST IMPORtant request a six-year-old Maanzi made of his cousin Zuri, who was also six. These two Ugandan children had been born to two brothers, who belonged to a rural group of pastoralists and farmers. Their village was more than fifty kilometres from the nearest town, where water ran in taps, roads had patches of tarmac and electricity was available only in major government buildings and houses. In the city, a few rich people and public servants also lived in houses with electricity and landline phones. In this village, life was very basic but not primitive: Both cows and people shared the same source of drinking water, and both drank it unboiled. When children took down the cows, sheep and goats to the stream to water them, they would also take a moment to kneel and drink a few handfuls of the same water. Down the stream, women and children could be seen fetching water to take home to prepare meals, oblivious of the pollution that was being done to it from the cows upstream.

Women spent time at home raising children and growing a few food crops around the homesteads, while men spent long hours in the wilderness taking care of their few long-horned cows, which were a source of prestige and the means to pay for a bride. In this village, like many rural areas, the roads were small winding footpaths, and few people could afford bicycles.

Their homes were built out of mud and wattle, and the majority of young children in the village did not wear clothes on a regular basis unless it was to go for church or there was a ceremony of sorts. And if the child was old enough and lucky to be attending school, they had the privilege of adorning their school uniform on weekdays.

"Of course," Zuri replied.

Equally serious, she also asked, "Will you take care of my daughter?"

"Always!" Maanzi replied, with a look that said he was slightly offended that she would have asked. They were friends from the beginning.

But that was their ritual. Every time one of them fell ill, the other took care of the toys. Maanzi took care of Zuri's dolls, that were made of dry banana leaves while she in turn shielded his herd of clay cattle from the rain.

Eighteen years later, Maanzi answered the phone and heard a woman crying on the other end. It was someone he had always held dear. Zuri wasn't physically ill this time, but he could sense the exhaustion and despair in her voice. She asked him the same question: "Will you take care of my daughter?"

Her name was Kesi. This child was a living, breathing nine-year-old.

Chapter 1

HIMA WAS A VILLAGE IN UGANDA, A SMALL COUNTRY IN EAST Africa. Cars were rarely seen in this part of the country and only came for one purpose: to buy the cows for beef and a few farm products to take to the towns. Hima was on a large plain surrounded by the foothills of a great mountain range in the southwestern part of Uganda.

The mountains surrounding this village were bare, with no trees on them; the men could see their herds of cattle from afar. They could also see if the cows were straying toward the lowlands where the crops were grown and move fast to go and deter them. In the cold months, the mountaintops were covered with thick fog every morning, and a thick cloud resting on the mountain in the evening was a herald for heavy rain either in the night or the next morning.

Most people were peasant farmers. A person was considered wealthy not by the size of his house or the clothes on his back but by the size of his herd of cattle. Because one needed cattle to get a wife for his son, and people gave out their daughters in marriage and in return got back cows for their family.

"We should finish our work so fast today," Maanzi told Zuri. He phrased it in a serious and calculated tone of voice, like a grown-up person. He was wearing an old, tattered pair of shorts with bare patches exposing his bottoms to the warm breeze.

"Why? Do you have somewhere to go, or is one of your cows giving birth today?" Zuri replied innocently, straightening her back, looking up into the sky and letting the warm breeze go over her face and kinky hair. She looked at her cousin's exposed bottoms through the torn shorts and smiled.

"What are you smiling at?" Maanzi asked with a confused look on his face.

"You really need another pair of shorts, you know," Zuri replied.

"So why do we have to get our work done early today?"

"Today there is a meeting at the church grounds, and I hear some important people are coming there. There will be many cars, well-dressed people and all. We should go and see them," Maanzi replied with an enthusiasm in his voice that left Zuri wondering what was exciting her friend.

"Let's figure out a plan; you know our mothers won't let us go," Zuri advised him. They both agreed that it was time to go and fetch some firewood from the bushes. So, they went on to let this plan be known to their parents (mothers).

"We are going to fetch firewood. Bye!" Maanzi announced to his mom hurriedly, running so fast lest she notice that there was already enough firewood for the day and asks him to stay and look after his young siblings or watch the pot of beans cooking on the fire.

He headed towards where his cousin was waiting and they beelined for the nearby bushes to get a few pieces of firewood to later act as their excuse for not being seen around their home for a while. After gathering a sizable bundle of dry pieces of wood for each, the two children headed for the church grounds at a fast speed. They had heard the sound of a few cars drive by the small roads while they were deep in the woods, collecting firewood.

At the meeting, all adults huddled together under a big tree, listening to a well-dressed man. He was the representative of the new government that had just come into power. The children were told to be silent, and if anyone so much as coughed, they were met with stern glares, yet not a word of admonition. On this day, the silence was of utmost importance, as something big was to be announced. The rebel army had been advancing and had taken over the capital. The ousted dictator had supposedly fled to a neighbouring country, and the new former rebel leader was announcing his agenda. He had a lot to say.

This government official, in a very calming and eloquent manner, started to address the people. The adults knew this man; he had been opposing the previous government and had left home to join the rebel group to fight, and for a while, most in this village thought he had been killed in battle, given that he had never returned home, not even once. It had been years.

He told the crowd that although the new government had come to power by a coup d'état, it was necessary. However, he pledged that the plan was to transition the country into a democracy as soon as possible, beginning with allowing people in the communities to elect their own representatives. He promised to improve social services, such as health care and housing that had been destroyed by the war. However, he stressed that even more urgent was the creation of a literate population. Education, he said, would lead to an improved standard of living for the whole population. But even more importantly, he said, "Education is of utmost importance so that everyday people can challenge the country's leadership and make the person in power accountable."

While other children were smitten by the army cars that these officials had come with, Zuri and Maanzi climbed the trees to catch a glimpse of the man who was talking, his voice confident, authoritative, and powerful, like nothing that they had ever heard. His words were moving and full of hope.

"Can you see him?" Maanzi asked Zuri, as they both hang from tree branches and peeping through the leaves to catch a glimpse of this powerful guest.

"Is that the new president?" Zuri asked.

"Yes, he is," answered Maanzi.

We could be like that man one day, if what he says is true—that we all shall go to school, Maanzi thought to himself, a little confused that he could think of a different life than the one he was having, the one he was used to, than the one his parents, uncles, and grandparents had known: looking after cows, little or no education, no opportunities.

Maanzi was still lost in his many thoughts, having a daydream, when Zuri interrupted," Hey, what is he saying?" I can barely hear him. Zuri was tagging and pulling on Maanzi's shorts.

Maanzi looked down at his cousin and responded, "quiet!"

The gentleman continued, "Education is the only way to ensure that history will not repeat itself. Parents, you all will be required to send your children to school. The girls will have the same opportunity to receive the same education as the boys because our population could not become independent when half of it cannot tell how much sugar costs."

Maanzi was so much pleased with what the gentleman was saying; he turned excitedly to Zuri and said, "Did you hear that? Even girls will be allowed to go to school with boys."

"So? What does that have to do with me?" asked Zuri.

"Silly! It means that you and I will go to the same school, get the same education, and one day, we could be here working for the government and driving those cars," Maanzi replied.

"And you could buy new trousers," Zuri replied and giggled as she looked at her cousin's torn old pair of shorts.

Maanzi and Zuri's fathers (Francis and Jackson) were among the crowd that had gathered for this meeting. This was one of several meetings that had been held that week throughout the country by government representatives. The president himself did give a similar speech to the nation over the radio, but this was heard by a few people in the country who could afford one. The speeches made by these government representatives across the country were met with great applause. The people were hopeful; you could hear the joy as the villagers walked past the farms. A few days after the meeting, Maanzi wanted answers from his father.

"Dad, do you think the well-dressed gentleman was serious about sending all the children, boys and girls, to school?" Maanzi asked.

It was in the middle of the day, the sun was scorching hot, and they were driving their small family herd of cows to the stream. The herd was for Maanzi's grandfather (Francis's Father), and as such, it belonged to the whole extended family, who took turns to take care of these few cows.

"Sure, why not?" Francis replied to his son, but he seemed to be preoccupied with something on his mind that day. Maanzi was unaware that his father was looking at him keenly, as he spoke on and on about the gentleman who spoke with authority and power.

"Do you know the gentleman who was speaking, Dad? If I can go to school, I will grow up to be like him. He spoke like a god; you know, I thought he was the president, but then I heard you and Uncle Jackson saying that he was just a representative of the government."

Maanzi could not hide the curiosity, excitement, and hopefulness that this speech sparked in him.

His father answered, "I know the gentleman who was giving the speech."

"Really?" Maanzi replied, curious. "Who is he? Are you friends?"

Francis replied, "His name is Jimmy. He comes from the neighbouring village. Your Uncle Jackson and I were friends with him growing up, looking after cows together in the bush every day. And one day ..." There was a slight pause in his speech, as if he was avoiding the next words, or as if he was in deep thought. Francis gave a loud shout at a cow that was straying from the path.

"And ... one day, what happened?" Maanzi asked.

Francis continued, "His father was the county chief, so he sent him off to school in the city. He studied and became a teacher, taught for a while in the city and married a nurse. They simply lived there. He returned and took his parents to live with him. We heard that he had joined the rebels fighting for a better government."

"Dad, are you sad?" asked Maanzi.

"No, son. It was good to see him after such a long time. And yes, what he was saying is true. Education will change our country; see what he has become? I barely recognized him. We grew up with him, ate raw mangoes in the bush together, and we talked about going to school a lot. He was lucky to get schooling while we did not. But now that the new government is talking about allowing every child to go to school for free, I think things will be different. If the new president has men like Jimmy, he has good men.

"Life will surely be better for our children than it was for us," Francis concluded. And there was silence between the two for the rest of the afternoon. As though each of them was pondering, what it could be, and what needed to be done next.

But one could also hear the occasional skeptic say, "How can you believe the words of a politician?" However, even the strongest skeptic was silenced when one year later, for the first time in Hima, a kindergarten school was opened. The president had kept his word. It is not that the president opened this school, it was because of the waves of hope, and the new government talking about and promoting education throughout the country that people in their own villages started to use their churches or even their own compounds, under trees to let the young children start school, who would otherwise have to wait until they would be old enough to walk very many kilometres to the few traditional primary schools that were available at the time.

Chapter 2

ZURI AND MAANZI WERE THE FIRST CHILDREN OF BROTHERS Jackson and Francis. Growing up in the same homestead, playing together all day long, going to fetch water and firewood, and doing similar chores in each of their homes gave them a sense of comradeship. They were friends.

They shared the burden of helping their mothers with their younger siblings and suffered the same degree of discipline if they did not perform according to the homestead rules. Their houses were about fifty feet from one another. There were several other houses in the neighbourhood; they belonged to their grandfather and the other uncles. It was customary for young men to build their own small mud and wattle houses around their parents' homes when they became adolescents. This prepared them for marriage, which usually took place soon because they were expected to follow this route to maintain a growing tribe.

The houses were arranged in a row. They all faced east and had one common compound that served as a large playground for all the children in the homestead. Behind each house was a vegetable garden for that household. Here the mothers grew food that would feed their families.

The houses basically had the same structure: a grass roof with walls made of mud and wattle and floors made from firmly pressed dirt. Still, their mothers raised a lot of dust when they swept the floors.

A little further off, about two kilometres away at the foothills of the mountain, was the expanse of land where Maanzi's and Zuri's fathers had each inherited an acre from their father. On this property, each brother kept a few cattle or cultivated plantain that would be used for food and some sold for income. This property had been the cause of many quarrels between the brothers, as each accused the other of moving the boundary stone from time to time.

Zuri was the eldest of seven children, three girls and four boys. She had been named by the traditional Swahili midwife because of the way she had come—after fourteen hours of labour. Her mother had lost a lot of blood, and she and the baby were in danger. Eventually, Zuri was born early in the morning. "Beautiful child, this one," the traditional midwife had said.

There was something special about Zuri. Although she had brown eyes and kinky black hair, like any other child in Hima, she had a beautiful dark-chocolate complexion. The midwife, who had learned her art in the neighbouring country of Tanzania and was fluent in Swahili, insisted that she be named Zuri, which means "beautiful," and that had stuck—a very rare name in a community where the people did not speak Swahili at all.

Maanzi was the eldest of nine children. His mother named him "brave one"; he had survived so many childhood illnesses and seemed to have a resilient trait, despite such adversity, even at a young age.

Maanzi and Zuri spent much of their waking hours together. By the standards of their community, their families were considered poor, but Maanzi and Zuri did not know any better, even though they wore tattered clothes and went barefoot. On a typical day in the village, they played together in the sand, helped take care of their younger siblings, and visited with the other children in the neighbourhood. After they walked kilometres under the scorching sun to get water from the well, they raced each other, laughing all the way back, while carrying their small pails, spilling half the water (to the dismay of their mothers).

Chapter 3

WITH THE NEW DISPENSATION OF EVERY VILLAGE ELECTING their own leaders, the rural people were excited to participate.

"I propose that Jackson be our local council," a member of the congregation suggested.

"No, sir," replied the modulator, who had been brought in from the next village to help conduct the election process in a democratic way.

"Why not?" the person asked.

"We'd like him to lead us." The village person insisted.

"Because this government wants to promote education and literacy, and Mr. Jackson does not know how to write." The modulator responded and ignored this contribution as he pointed out to another man who had his hand up to propose a candidate for another post.

Jackson and his brother Francis were seated next to each other. Jackson, a hot-tempered man who liked to fight for respect and dignity, could not take this insult, so he stood up and left, without saying a word. His face and demeanour showed that he was very mad. The meeting ended without electing anyone, which frustrated the village folks.

Jackson came to Francis's house that evening, still angry. His brother's family were all seated on the ground except the head of the house, who sat on a round wooden stool, eating from the same flat plate.

"Would you like to eat with us?" Francis asked.

"No, thank you, we just finished eating at my house," replied Jackson. "So who did that educated man choose to be our chairperson?" he asked, with anger still in his voice. "The meeting ended without us agreeing on someone," Francis replied. "We will have to look around for a person who can help us develop."

"This new government is no different from the past one," Jackson complained. "All they care about is themselves. They say it will be a democracy, and yet they are telling us who should be leading us, who not to elect, and calling us names, uneducated, can you imagine that eh?"

"Well, I guess now we know that the future is in education. Did you see how Jimmy turned out?" Francis asked calmly. Trying to lighten his brother's foul mood.

"Have a good night then," Jackson said as he left his brother's house.

The village finally chose a leader and a committee of elders who would lead and guide them. Jackson was selected to the committee, which pleased him so much, but Francis was not.

"Now this government knows that we have sense in what we say and influence in this community," Jackson was heard telling a neighbour after being allowed on the committee.

Each village now had a committee that would address the local problems of the community, and if these were too great, they would be resolved at the sub-county level, then county level and finally at a district level.

The newly formed village committee was tasked with improving education. This was crucial, as most of the committee members had young children of their own. Prior to this, the children had to wait until they were old enough to walk the five or six kilometres to the nearest primary school. This resulted in children starting school when they were much older or not at all for most of the girls. By then it would be too late because they would be adolescents and plans to marry them off would have begun.

Mr. Ntare was an elderly gentleman who had worked for the previous chief's household. He had been involved in looking after Jimmy's fathers' household and knew something about the benefits of education. He had watched the chief hire teachers from the city to come and coach his children. While he had basic education himself, he had good insight and was respected as an advocate for child education. His grandchildren were among the few children in the village who were going to a primary school, and others had in fact joined secondary school in the big town. He was sent by the committee to approach Miss Nkwanzi about the possibility of teaching the nursery school that would be meeting at the local church grounds.

Miss Nkwanzi was slender; her hair fell to her shoulders when combed out, but she preferred to keep it in locks, so it was easily managed. She only had formal training up to Primary Four, but still, this was rare for a woman in this community. One of her older brothers had refused to go to school without her, complaining that she had all the fun because she stayed home and didn't have to be disciplined by teachers. He wouldn't go to school if she didn't as well. Her father relented and let her go to school, but by the time she reached Primary Four, her mother had other children and needed her help, so her schooling ended abruptly.

The news of the start of kindergarten school was made at church following the service. Later, Mr. Ntare and his committee secretary, Mr. Muntu, went door to door. All children regardless of their age and gender were encouraged to attend the new school as long as they could walk there and back. There would be no classroom, desks, or chairs in this school. The students were to sit on the verandah at the entrance of the church. There would be a small fee to cover the little writing boards the students would use. Miss Nkwanzi would bring a large blackboard with her each morning. The majority of the parents in the community rushed to enroll their children in the school. The ages varied from four to ten years. Eventually, more and more parents enrolled their children in the new school, including the girls.

Maanzi and Zuri were among the first children enrolled in the new kindergarten. At six years old, they were the youngest in the group of pupils. They could not contain their excitement as they waited for the first day of school, if only because that meant they no longer had to do as many household chores.

"You have a new shirt for school tomorrow," Maanzi's mother announced.

He was very excited that he would be putting on a clean shirt every day. It was hand-sewn from an extra piece of his mother's cloth, and he loved it.

At the school, Maanzi and Zuri met other children from their village. They spent much of the day playing after writing their numbers and memorizing the alphabet. Maanzi would repeat whatever he had learned at school that day to his mother, who was keen to listen but also because she was with him as they did their house chores.

The school subjects were math and English, but Zuri loved the stories the teacher told at the end of each day best of all. They were mostly around the subjects integrated with the lessons about good morals, acceptable culture, and social norms. Maanzi was simply happy that they got to meet other children, sing, play, and write in the sand. Occasionally, there were no school supplies, so the students were told to draw with their fingers in the sand, and when their teacher had looked at all their drawings, they would wash off their work from the sand with their hands and start off another lesson.

They spent time discussing the highlights that happened at school as they did their chores.

Chapter 4

AFTER ALMOST A YEAR IN KINDERGARTEN, MAANZI AND ZURI were ready to start primary school. They were both still younger than the other students who went to primary school from their village. This new school was about four to five kilometres from home. This meant waking up early; there was little time for breakfast (usually a concentrated cup of boiled cow's milk and occasionally homemade yogurt) to be at school on time. Breakfast was not an everyday thing. When milk was available, they had breakfast, but in the months that the local cows were not in season to produce milk, the children went without breakfast or simply ate leftover food from the night. Food was never enough to be leftover after a meal.

They had to walk in the frigid morning, barefooted, and their tattered clothes were no match for the weather conditions.

The two children would come home from school and do their chores right away; they would then go to bed, very tired. With no alarm clocks, the two depended on their parents to wake them.

One day, Maanzi knocked on the door of his uncle, Jackson. Zuri's mom came out and said, "Zuri came to your house and knocked but you did not answer. She left; she must be nearing school now. You will have to run as fast as you can to make it there on time."

Filled with fear about the punishment for being late and angry at his cousin for leaving him asleep, Maanzi started to run toward school, all the while crying aloud.

While he was at least a hundred meters away, the bell rang; every child ran and lined up.

Phew, I have made it, Maanzi thought.

As he lined up, a sense of doom came over him immediately; every other child was holding up pieces of dry banana leaves. Their school had dry banana leaves for a roof, and each of them had to routinely bring a bundle for the roofing especially in the rainy season. Maanzi was distraught, and with his face glued to the floor, hoping that the ground could swallow him, his dreaded scenario ensued.

"Maanzi, where is your bundle of banana leaves?" asked one of the school prefects. "All those without the banana leaves, come forward," the prefect demanded, as the teacher on duty was standing in front, with itching hands holding a cane.

"You lazy children, come forward and I will teach you a lesson," the teacher demanded. One by one, the children prostrated before their teacher and received their lashes on their bottoms and then went back into their lines.

Maanzi received ten lashes for this.

"Now, you all remember that we asked you to bring cow dung for pressing the floor of our classrooms since today is Friday," one of the teachers said. "Those of you who do not have the cow dung, come forward."

Maanzi was still crying from the previous lashes; he came forward, still sobbing.

"If you fear to be punished, you should obey the rules and bring whatever we ask for," the teacher yelled.

"Your tears are not cow dung; get on the ground." He gave him ten more lashes.

Maanzi was having a really bad day and began rethinking this school thing. It was time for class to begin. He had spent the last evening taking care of cows, and there had been no time to do his homework. As he sat down on the papyrus carpet that the school used for covering the dusty floors, a sense of doom was mounting.

"We are going to start reviewing our abacus homework," the teacher announced. "Please pass your books to your neighbour, and you will mark each other. The answers are going to be on the front blackboard."

Maanzi was in tears again. His book was empty; the homework was not done.

"Excuse me, teacher," the child next to Maanzi said, raising his hand.

"Yes, what is it?" asked the teacher.

"Maanzi has no homework to mark," replied the student.

"What? Come over here," the teacher said as he walked to the opposite corner of the classroom to pick up a cane from a bundle that he kept there.

"Please don't beat him again," a familiar voice spoke from the middle of the classroom.

Everybody turned to see where this voice was coming from and for what reason.

"He was very sick last evening. Maanzi was very sick, and that's why he had no banana leaves or cow dung." It was Zuri, pleading for her friend.

"Well, okay, I will forgive him for today," said the teacher. "Bring your homework on Monday."

"Thank you, thank you," Maanzi said as he looked at his cousin.

The teacher replied, "You are welcome," as though this was directed to him.

Maanzi was very grateful for a friend like Zuri, and as they went home that afternoon, he turned to her and whispered again,

"Thank you. I do not want to go back to school anymore. The punishment is getting worse, and I can barely sit on my bottom."

"But you told me that if we study hard, we could be like that gentleman who represents the government or be like Miss Nkwanzi," Zuri replied.

And so, day after day, the resentment for school grew; though they still loved the classwork, they dreaded each day and were terrified of the teacher's punishments.

Their parents both believed that the teachers only had their children's best intentions at heart, and Zuri and Maanzi would rather bite their tongues than confess that they had been disciplined at school, lest it result in further disciplinary measures at home. Soon the majority of their conversations were to devise schemes to avoid school punishment.

The two soon learned that one could hide and play in the nearby shrubs until lunchtime and then join in on the afternoon classes, after which they would go home with the other children from their neighbourhood as though they had studied all day. This was possible as many children missed school from time to time because of many reasons, such as illnesses, lack of books or their parents simply wanted them home to help with some house chores. And as long as the parents did not come to school complaining, the teachers did not care to ask why children did not come to school. The classes were also big, with more than thirty or more children for one teacher, crowded in one room.

It was also common for two classes to share a single classroom. So the two groups would sit in the same room facing opposite directions, taking different classes, with two teachers each shouting out instructions at the pupils.

However, as bad luck would have it, a distant friend of their parents taught a different class in the same school. One morning he came looking for them because he wanted them to deliver a message to Maanzi's father. Needless to say, he delivered the message himself that both children were not in school that day.

The two were not at home that evening when their teacher showed up. "Good evening," he said. Francis rushed outside of the kitchen and gave him a hug. "It's good to see you, it has been a while. How are you doing?"

"Please have a seat," Francis was handing over a wooden three-legged stool to him.

"How are your son and your brother's daughter doing?" the teacher and guest enquired.

"They are very well, thank you for asking; they seem to like school so much. In fact, they just returned from school a few hours ago."

"But they were not in school today, or even yesterday. I looked for them to give them this letter from your old friend but could not find them."

"Really? They went to school yesterday and today," Francis said, confused.

Having had little formal education himself, more than anything, he was determined that it would be different for his child, so Francis decided he was going to start escorting them to school every day, as long as he could.

After supper, that night, Maanzi's father called him and said, "Come with me to Uncle Jackson's house."

"Why? Is anything wrong?" he asked. He knew something was going down from the tone of his father's voice.

Francis led him silently to his brother's house.

"These two have not been attending school," he said when they got to Jackson's house. "I do not know where they spend their days."

The three parents asked in unison, "Why were you not at school today? And, where were you?"

The two friends looked down on the floor and said nothing.

"Well, each of you will receive twenty lashes, now!" Francis said.

They each received their punishment and ran outside into the dark, in pain but managing to giggle.

"We are busted," Zuri said.

"I am tired of the beating at school; we have to think of something else," Maanzi said.

"We have all weekend to think about it," Zuri reassured him.

"Goodnight," Maanzi said. Then he left his cousin and headed back to their house.

Since that plot failed, Maanzi and Zuri devised other plans to avoid school. One day, after returning from school while they went to fetch water, they agreed to fall sick that night. So upon arriving home that evening, Maanzi acted unwell. He had a dry cough and withdrew from all conversation. Meanwhile, Zuri was also putting on a show. She noticeably ate very little dinner. Kesiime, her mother, asked, "What's the problem?"

"I do not feel well," Zuri said. "I think I have a fever, cold, and headache."

"Oh, I'm sorry about that," she replied, touching her forehead. "You do seem unwell and may have to stay home from school tomorrow. Maybe tomorrow you could watch the children for me while I go to the garden since that will not tire you too much."

Zuri did not reply but was inwardly delighted, as she would much rather watch the children for one day; if only she could avoid being disciplined at school.

Francis, on the other hand, eyed his son curiously after observing that Maanzi had not engaged in any conversation, as he usually did. He asked his wife, Grace, "Where is that reusable syringe and needle?"

"Why do you want them?" Grace replied.

"I should boil them and give Maanzi a penicillin injection. He seems to be unwell, and it would be better to treat him early so that he can recover faster and not have to miss many school days.

He is quite small, and each illness farther weakens him. We don't want him to become too ill."

Because Maanzi was terrified of injections, he immediately recovered. He was lying down on the grass on the floor of their kitchen, all the while coughing every few minutes and projecting a very ill demeanour. The coughing ceased, he sat right upright and he regaled them with colourful stories about a boy who peed in his pants while standing in front of the class, because he was afraid that the teacher would discipline him.

Very early the next morning, as Maanzi prepared to go to school, Zuri was still coughing.

"Well, your cousin is very unwell," Francis said, "so you will have to go to school on your own today."

So Maanzi and Francis made their daily trek to school. Zuri had successfully avoided school, faking illness with no consequences.

Soon, even Zuri's mother became aware of their schemes. But that did not stop them from trying. Maanzi feigned illness, and when he agreed to be taken to the nurse, his father took his sickness seriously.

They soon began to take turns about who was to fall ill; the conversations between them were whispered tensely.

"There is no way I am going to go to school tomorrow without you," Zuri said. "You have to come with me; you are not sick," she continued. "Tomorrow is my day. You have taken two days in a row; it's not fair. We were supposed to alternate days."

"But I am more ill than you are," Maanzi replied.

"Sickness does not take turns. You are either sick or not sick," Maanzi continued. "I am even planning on getting another injection tonight, which will prove to my father that I am really very ill, see?" Maanzi said, giggling.

Unknown to them, as the two friends were behind the kitchen, shelling beans from their pods for supper, Maanzi's mum was in the kitchen, listening in on their conversation.

Grace cleared her throat and said, "From now on, both of you will be attending school, every day, every weekday. Your only days off will be when the school closes. What kind of a game are you two playing? Do you think I enjoy doing all the work alone at home while you go to school every day? This word will reach your fathers tonight, and you will find out the consequences later."

So that was the end of that.

Chapter 5

WITH EACH PASSING YEAR IN PRIMARY SCHOOL, MAANZI AND ZURI learned to navigate the school system and cover for each other. Being older, they could walk faster and get to school on time. Therefore, school was a bit more bearable. Or maybe they both realized that they would have no choice but to bear it. Whatever the case, they both slowly began to appreciate the math, science, English, and history that they were taught and began to realize that they could have a better life than their parents had. Maanzi was excited about the history class, because they talked about the humble beginnings of the current government leaders, how they had fought for democracy, and how they were pro-people, education, and development. He had seen and listened to one of these men first-hand and admired what he had become.

Zuri, the more studious of the two, and a newly elected class prefect decided that she wanted to be a teacher. So much so she renamed her dolls after one of the teachers and would spend her spare time instructing the dolls or her unwilling younger cousins and siblings to stand in an orderly line:

"Line up properly and repeat after me: A, E, I, O, U ... 1, 2, 3 ... You come here, you have not done your homework, ten lashes for you. And do not be shedding tears for me, your tears won't write your homework." Zuri would do this with her dolls, even in the absence of other people.

Maanzi, on the other hand, aspired to be a cattle keeper, like the rest of the men in his family, but he also wanted to study and become informed. He knew he wanted something different, but he was not sure what yet.

Of course, they were still plagued with school woes, the worst of which happened every Friday morning. This ritual was a result of the initiative of the new government to improve health in the communities.

So, in addition to what they were taught in school, every Friday morning, the lower primary classes would have to have a mandatory check to assess personal hygiene. This was done by the class prefects, who would report to the teachers. The check included assessing finger- and toenails for jiggers and hair for lice.

As fate would have it, Zuri received a clean bill of health from another prefect. However, when she turned to check Maanzi, she whispered, "You have a jigger growing on your third toe."

A jigger infection, known as tungiasis, is an inflammatory skin disease caused by a flea (also known as chigoe flea, nigua, or sand flea).

He looked down with shame and embarrassment. The punishment for having a jigger was a bit dramatic; you would have it removed by a safety pin, and red pepper would be crushed and put in the fresh wound, which would set you crying, wiggling your toes, scratching the ground in front of your peers, usually sending them into fits of laughter. He knew because he had been one of the others who had laughed.

"I am not going to tell anyone," Zuri whispered. "But when we get home, you should ask your mum to get it out as soon as possible."

"Thank you, thank you, thank you." Maanzi's voice quivered as he stared at her, eyes filled with gratitude.

"Always," she smiled and sweetly replied, moving on to the next person.

About this point, the new minister of agriculture had been announced on the radio. But this particular announcement caused a stir in the country. While the man was undoubtedly well educated, he wasn't suitable because his background training was law. Being a new post, the people of Hima did not quite understand why they even needed a minister of agriculture.

"I get up each morning and go to my garden and dig. So why do we need someone to tell us what we already know?" Jackson asked angrily. "See, I told you this new president is up to no good. Besides, he is even a lawyer; what does he know about farming?"

"Daddy, what is a lawyer?" asked Maanzi, who was keenly listening in on the conversation.

"But you never went to school, and you know about planting crops and rearing cattle," Francis replied, ignoring Maanzi's question. "Even this new minister doesn't need to go to school."

The argument between the brothers became heated.

"I know because I grew up farming. It was my school from an early age. This man just went to school."

"These men have good ideas, and maybe that's what we need for development," Francis replied.

"You think if we keep our children busy with school, they will know anything about cows when they grow up?" Jackson asked as if to suggest that they should stop sending their children to school.

"Maanzi, please go ahead and see if there is water in the troughs to water the cows," Francis instructed his son.

Later that day, as they looked after the cows, his father explained that a lawyer was someone who defended people who could not defend themselves. This explanation resonated with him, and once again, he felt that he wanted to do that, not knowing why at the time. It was then that he resolved to study hard to become one of those; unlike the man on the radio, he vowed not to change his profession, even if called to be a minister. Francis looked at Maanzi as though understanding that he meant what he said, with an expression of resolve to help his son achieve his dreams in spite of his own dwindling finances.

With a new determination for education, Maanzi knew that he wanted to study and change his life. He wanted to be in a position to defend people. But on days, when he would be in the wilderness looking after the cows with other children from his village, they would look up into the sky and see a plane dirt across the sky and he would dream that maybe one day, he could become a pilot.

Hey guys, "do you ever wonder what it would feel like to enter a plane or even just touch it?" Maanzi asked one day.

To this, his friends would laugh so hard and dismiss him as a daydreamer.

"Who in your family has been to the city or been to college or owns a bicycle?" once one of his friends asked sarcastically. Maanzi knew that the odds were against him, but he dared to hope. "My parents will get the money," he thought to himself.

"I think I will become a pilot one day. And when I fly across this village, I will look down and wave at you down here, or even throw some food down for you." Maanzi insisted.

"Yeah, and we will be living in the president's house," one of his fellow children joked sarcastically.

Maanzi was about to meet with a distant cousin of Francis for the first time. Jay was putting himself through college to become a teacher. Uncle Jay believed in education, and though Francis was finding it difficult to take Maanzi through school, he was working hard to change that narrative and looking for alternative strategies.

That is when Francis had reached out to his cousin Jay.

Chapter 6

MAANZI WAS INTRODUCED TO HIS UNCLE JAY AT A TIME WHEN HE was in dire need of help. It was a common class joke that Maanzi was always among those that the teacher would send home for not paying their school fees.

"This school is only for those who can afford to pay," a teacher announced one day. "The government pays our salaries, but your parents should contribute by paying fees and buying all you need. Do not come back unless you have the money."

This was before primary school was universally free; there was no free school. Some of the students would giggle as Maanzi rushed out of his class, conflicted. He was ashamed every time this happened.

"Who has not paid fees again," some of his classmates would whisper from the back as the teacher stood in front of the class with the list of school-fees defaulters.

Maanzi would begin to gather his books, even before his name would be read. He knew that his parents had not been able to raise the money.

He was angry that his father could never afford school fees, but soon he would stoop his head in sorrow. His father was trying. Maanzi knew this. Francis had many mouths to feed, and he had no formal employment. *"I was beginning to like school since it will one day be the only way to escape this shame and ridicule,"* Maanzi thought to himself as he walked home. *"I will give anything to stay in school right now. It is the only way out of this life, the shame, the ridicule and embarrassment."* He continued to get lost in his thoughts; tears were rolling down his face as he headed back home in the midmorning hours. He now considered the teachers' discipline more welcome than having to miss school and go back home.

He arrived home, just in time to find his siblings crying and his mother in dire need of an extra hand.

"They sent you back?" she asked her son.

"Please go and remove your uniform and come out here and help me with the children. The other one has pooped in his clothes," his mother continued oblivious of the sadness on Maanzi's face that day. He changed from his uniform and immediately drained his thoughts and frustration in helping his mother with his siblings.

Francis soon found a perfect solution to this, at least for a while. When he returned home that evening, after supper, his son narrated the old same story about unpaid dues and how he was sent home from school again.

Francis listened attentively, looking strained, he paused for a while and then gave a look to his wife and then turned to his son.

"You will be living with your Uncle Jay for a while," he told Maanzi.

"He will come here tomorrow evening to pick you up," Francis continued and looked away from his son.

There had been a meeting between his parents and Uncle Jay. They decided it was best that he lives with his uncle, and he wasn't given any time to object.

"He is a teacher and will help you," Grace said, consoling Maanzi.

Maanzi was only vaguely aware of his Uncle Jay until the evening he arrived to pick him up. Uncle Jay was at least twenty-five, had a slim build, and was five feet seven inches tall. He had a square jaw and was considered very handsome. He was a self-determined, self-motivated person. For some reason, he wanted to learn more, even after being married, which in this rural population meant settling down, looking after a few cows, cultivating your piece of land for food and rearing children. He looked for more opportunities to attain a higher level of education. He would take Maanzi to the same schools in which he tutored as a student-teacher.

"Hello, little Maanzi," he said.

"My name is Uncle Jay; you will be living with me from now on. Go get your things ready, we are leaving soon." He didn't have much to pack.

Jay and Francis sat on wooden stools in the compound under a tree and continued an adult conversation in hush-hush voices.

Maanzi's mother, though having prior knowledge of the arrangements, seemed disturbed by this moment. Where she normally would have let him pack his clothes, this time she followed him into the bedroom. She held him close, and he could hear her sniffing above his head.

"You behave and work hard," she said. "I won't be around to tell you what to do, so listen to your uncle and do as he says.

"Promise me that you will work hard and become the person that you want to be." Grace wiped away her tears with a scarf.

"I don't want to go," he said.

"Why? Why am I going away?"

Maanzi was crying unashamedly, not caring that his younger siblings saw him and may laugh at him later because of this display of emotion. His mother, however, did not reply but went back to preparing an early evening meal for the family to eat with Uncle Jay.

Maanzi had one last good-bye, so he walked to Zuri's house, dreading each step yet knowing that he must. He had never known a life without her in it. They played together, studied together, conspired together, dreamed together and aspired together; this was soon to end, but he didn't quite understand why.

Maanzi was headed to parts unknown, with people previously unknown, hoping that the person taking him was a good person.

"There is a man at our house called Uncle Jay," Maanzi started. "He is here to take me with him. I don't want to go but my parents have already decided. My books are packed. I wanted to come and say goodbye and ask that you can take care of my 'cows'."

After he told his friend he was leaving, Zuri was inconsolable as she cried into the sleeve of her blouse. She looked away and became emotional and was shaking uncontrollably with a grief-stricken face.

"You'll get new friends and forget me," she said, sniffing.

"No, I won't," he replied. "I'll ask Uncle Jay to bring me home often to see you."

"He won't let you," was her reply.

"How do you know?" he replied.

"You don't really know him," Zuri responded. He is a stranger, why do you have to go with him, and today?" she demanded.

Zuri continued, "When people leave, they don't come back. Don't you remember Charles? It's been three years, and he is still not back." Charles was one of their distant cousins. He was a son of their uncle from another wife of their paternal grandfather, who was picked by a good Samaritan, a friend of his father who lived in the city to go and stay with him, help him with running daily errands in his hardware shop in return for school fees. The three had been friends, and they had shared the childhood bond of dreaming about a different life. Charles was now attending school during day time and working at his father's friend's shop in the evenings, weekends, and holidays.

I will come back, he vowed silently but then said aloud, "It will be different this time."

The two friends embraced, cried, and said their good-byes.

"Maanzi, Maanzi, where are you?" his mother called out.

"I am coming," Maanzi replied. He forced his feet to walk away from Zuri, and he felt as though he was having a heart attack.

Life is so unfair. Why do I have to leave my friend alone? Who will protect her, and who will look out for me, defend me before the teachers?

His mind was racing, troubled with thoughts of parting with his friend and companion.

Chapter 7

ZURI STAYED IN THE HOMESTEAD WHERE THEY BOTH GREW UP. She continued to go to the same primary school, where she was an excellent student. She had the same routine, although her chores increased. With each additional sibling that was born in the successive years, she had to take care and watch over them. The household need for water increased and being the eldest child, this meant more trips to the well for her. Besides, she was of an age to help her mother with the more challenging chores, such as washing the clothes, planting food crops, and cooking. As a result, she started to miss more school.

Maanzi was taken to live with Uncle Jay. Because of his education, he was well-spoken and well respected in the community, even though he was just starting in his career. His opinion was greatly valued when people discussed the news. But as Maanzi had begun to realize, it was because of his love for education, his advocacy for children to go to school, and his desire to help children attain an education that he was respected.

At the time, Uncle Jay had a wife named Mary and a baby girl named Kemi. He was working as a student-teacher but was often transferred to a different school. He had settled his wife and child in a home about ten kilometres from Maanzi's home, just over the hills in an area that was mostly flat land and shrubs. Uncle Jay had a large plot of land and a larger house than Maanzi's parents. Aunt Mary had a garden behind the house and a much larger one a little farther off; she employed some people from the village to help her till the land. Her workers usually were fellow women from the same village or the surrounding villages who had insufficient produce from their gardens. They worked to earn additional food to feed their families.

Uncle Jay lived in the schoolhouse during the school term and only went back to his home during the school holidays. The college and the schools that Uncle Jay went to were also far away from his home village. Maanzi would follow Uncle Jay wherever he went. They stayed together in the school housing, and whatever school Uncle Jay was transferred to, Maanzi went right along with him. Eventually, Maanzi attended five different schools over seven years.

Maanzi later learned why Uncle Jay changed schools so often. Sometimes it was because he was being moved by the college he attended, but most times he looked out for a school that paid a better stipend for him as a student teacher and yet still allowed him to attend college over the weekend. Maanzi eventually also figured out why he had been sent to live with Uncle Jay. As a student teacher, one of the benefits included waiving school fees for your child. Maanzi had been introduced as his adopted son, which in essence he was. It was gracious of Uncle Jay to afford him the opportunity, and he was grateful for it (on most days).

On many lonely days, Maanzi would sit outside their school residential house, look into the sky and think of his home, and he would hope that Zuri was well and continuing to work hard toward her dream. He also discovered that looking up into the sky while lying on the ground, prevented tears from dripping down in those emotional moments, so this posture became his default whenever he was feeling low and missed his home and friend. That, however, motivated him to work harder. He began to understand that his family wanted him to succeed, but many times, that burden was a little too heavy to bear. On such days, he would go to the garden, hide behind the shrubs, and cry out loud into the nothingness of the sky. He was grateful, yes, he was. But he missed his home, he missed his parents and siblings, and he missed Zuri. Yes, he missed waiting on his siblings. Living in this new household, sometimes he felt as though he simply was the help.

Chapter 8

MAANZI WOULD STAY WITH UNCLE JAY AND HIS FAMILY DURING the holidays as well. Here again, he would have to get used to a new routine. He would rise at dawn with his uncle and aunt, and they would go to the farm first thing in the morning to work before the scorching sun came out and it was uncomfortable. Once this was done, they would all return home, and he was then sent out to fetch water for use in the home. Given that he was young and small in build, he preferred to carry smaller jerry cans, but this would mean that he had to go back and forth many times. After that, he would tend the goats in the afternoon and then watch Kemi, his cousin, in the evenings or whenever he was free. The meals were served twice a day, lunch and supper, as was common in rural communities.

One evening, during the holidays, while Uncle Jay was away, Maanzi was in the kitchen helping his aunt. It was after a particularly long day, and he was bone tired. Aunt Mary, however, was in a good mood and was telling him stories about growing up in her village. Maanzi looked at her; her nostalgic stories stirred up a longing in his heart. He knew the rules: You never ask for what you want, you wait until it's offered to you. But the stories she told of the different pranks she and her younger siblings played on each other made him think she would understand. So quietly, after a few minutes of silence, he dared to ask if he could go visit his family; his parents had not visited him in his new home, there were no phones at the time, and he missed his cousins and siblings terribly. Aunt Mary, who had been reminiscing, seemed to be jolted back to reality.

"No," she replied, and that was that.

"You know the rules. Your uncle would not allow that," Mary concluded.

Maanzi bowed his head, angry at himself for that moment of weakness that had caused him to ask and praying that he would not be punished for it.

In addition to educating Maanzi in school, Uncle Jay showed him how to work hard. He strove to support his young family while paying his college tuition fees. To make ends meet, on the weekends and holidays when he was home, he would borrow a bicycle from a friend and peddle bananas to the neighbouring towns; sometimes he would cycle fifty kilometres before someone would buy the bananas. Maanzi would always help with part of the journey and push the bicycle that was laden with produce, since the roads were difficult, and it was during these difficult journeys that the two finally bonded. One day, they left very early in the morning, around five o'clock.

"Maanzi, wake up, I need your help with the bicycle," Jay called out from outside the small room in his house.

Maanzi woke up and wrapped himself in an oversize old shirt of uncle Jay.

"How many bunches of matoke are you taking today?" Maanzi asked.

"I am taking four," Jay replied. It will be difficult to do, but we have no choice; the bicycle owner has asked that I return it this evening, and we will be returning to school soon. If I do not return the bicycle today, we may not be able to borrow it next time."

Maanzi was about ten years old; he held the bicycle, which was almost his height.

But after the first bunch of matoke went on, the bicycle was lifted off the ground, and everything came crashing down on top of the poor boy. One bunch of bananas was destroyed, and it was now unfit for sale.

"I am sorry, it is very heavy," Maanzi told his uncle.

"Don't be sorry," Uncle Jay said angrily.

"Your sorry is not going to bring back this spoilt bunch of matoke or mend the bicycle if you break it. Now, hold firm, and do not move."

With trembling arms, he loaded the three bunches onto the bicycle. Now began the journey of pushing the whole load through the path from Jay's home to the small road.

After a while, Uncle Jay said, "Let us stop and rest." After they carefully rested their banana-loaded bicycle against a big tree, the man and boy sat down under the cover of the dark. It would soon be dawn, and they had to be at the road where Jay would be able to start peddling.

There was silence. Maanzi wondered whether his uncle was still mad at him for failing to hold the bicycle still or if he had something on his mind.

"Uncle Jay, are you mad at me?" Maanzi asked.

As he looked into a distance, Jay held a piece of wood in his hands. Fidgeting with wood, he thought for a while before he broke it into pieces and turned to Maanzi.

"Maanzi, when you fall, do not ever stay down. Get yourself up; when you fail, try again, because it is your only alternative."

"No one sees your struggles, only the results: failure or success. Now let's push again." He stood up, cleaned the back of his tired-looking working trousers, and carefully got the loaded bicycle off the tree. Maanzi followed and started pushing at the back of the load.

Sounding short of breath, Jay started talking as they struggled to push their bicycle uphill, "Do not feel bad about the matoke bunch that got destroyed," he continued. "If I did not have you to help, I could never load this bicycle. We have to be grateful for these remaining three. No one sees us in this dark struggling, no one is here to help us, so if we fall, we have to stand again. We have to push ourselves or else nobody will. We are almost on the road. We are a team. Push more. And soon, they were at the road, the path where Jay could jump onto the bicycle and peddle away. There would be other hills to climb ahead, but Maanzi had to return home because his chores awaited him: goats, fetching water, and babysitting.

"Hold the bicycle for me; now, let go," Jay announced. The two parted ways, with no word.

Jay rode off on the bicycle. Maanzi went back home. He always wondered what Jay did with the hills along the way without him to help push or steady the bicycle for him. He listened carefully to every conversation and watched the man carefully as he struggled each day to provide for his family and prepare for the next school term. Maanzi was acutely aware of how his Uncle struggled to raise money to pay his tuition and support his young family who were left behind every school term with no help.

The next week would be one of their tough times. Another school term would be coming up. They would be trekking many kilometres for many hours to go to their school, and Jay would be preparing for college again.

The start of each school term was a busy affair in Uncle Jay's household. Since Maanzi and Uncle Jay lived in the staff housing during the school terms, Aunt Mary would prepare as much dried food to last the two of them as long as possible. Uncle Jay would again borrow a bicycle from a friend; he would place all their luggage on it, together with some bunches of bananas to sell along the way. Every space on the bicycle was filled, leaving no room for either Maanzi or Uncle Jay to sit. Instead, they spent much of the journey walking and pushing the bicycle and their luggage.

Their journey did not end after arriving at the school. Since Uncle Jay had borrowed the bicycle, he would ride it back and then walk back to school, usually on the same day to be with Maanzi. Life was what it was, and not one day did Maanzi see Uncle Jay complain. Uncle Jay had a goal he was aspiring to; he repeatedly said, "We have to work hard if we are to change our future."

That matter-of-fact attitude soon rubbed off on Maanzi as well. He knew what needed to be done, and he resolved to do it: work hard, study hard, keep moving forward, no complaining, and no crying about home. If only he could keep it all together all the time. But life, he discovered, would help him master these lessons.

Maanzi had only a few clothes (shoes were out of the question). He had his school uniform, which he used for the weekdays and another pair of home clothes for the weekend. Uncle Jay did not have many clothes either. He had two pairs of trousers and two shirts, and one pair of old shoes which had taken on a shape of their own and had holes underneath. Uncle Jay placed plastic inside his shoes to protect his feet from the holes on the soles. He, on the other hand, truly believed that cleanliness was next to godliness and that a clean mind dwells in a clean body, so they washed their school clothes each night and hung them to dry, ready for the next day. This was because they had just one outfit.

Meals were so inconsistent that Maanzi took to praying each night that he would have a meal the next day. Many times while the rest of the school broke off for lunch, Maanzi and Uncle Jay would go back to their schoolhouse of two rooms (a living room and a bedroom) and have a cup of black tea with no milk and no sugar or share a piece of cooked cassava. On occasion, when there wasn't enough food to share, Uncle Jay would give it to Maanzi, claiming that he didn't have to eat much. He would then make do with water or simply take a walk in the dark, claiming he needed to think. Maanzi never dared to ask his uncle where he went or what he had to think about. *He would imagine, though, that his uncle wondered whether any of the sacrifices they were making would ultimately pay off.* But in the little boy's mind, there were questions he dared not ask.

Why did his own family not help out and bring them food at school?

How come Uncle Jay did not reach out to his family as the situation grew dire?

Surely someone would help them out. But the school was more than forty kilometres from Uncle Jay's home, and none of his brothers had a bicycle to help bring the food. In Maanzi's mind, someone could at least borrow a bicycle and bring them some food from Uncle Jay's garden.

During those days, there was a lot of silence at Uncle Jay's schoolhouse. He would work on his lesson plans as Maanzi would work on his homework. The silence was pregnant with determination on both their parts. They would have to work hard and change their current situation, or they were doomed. Uncle Jay had a heavy load to bear; he was using his and his wife's meagre resources to go to school, which did not guarantee a better future for them. He was responsible for Maanzi and had promised to put him through primary school; however, the young boy was wasting away with no food to eat. If this education thing did not work out ... He would suddenly snap at Maanzi and tell him to hurry or else they would be late for the afternoon classes.

However, through it all, Uncle Jay was ever the optimistic one. He could not tolerate self-pity or despair. Every Saturday and Sunday, Uncle Jay walked along the dirt roads, paved with occasional shrubs and tall grass about a meter high, to and from his college. It was a three- to four-hour journey each way. Many days, he went without lunch.

During one of their long journeys back from school at the end of the term, the tiredness got the better of them, and they had a look of exhaustion on their faces. As if to lighten the moment, after a period of thoughtful silence, Uncle Jay, knowing that Maanzi was tired and hungry and pitying himself, asked, "Do you still want to be a lawyer?" his voice hoarse and barely above a whisper. He had to repeat the question before Maanzi heard what he was saying.

"No," Maanzi replied.

"What happened? Did you change your mind?" Jay asked.

Maanzi told his Uncle about an incident that happened to him a few years prior when he fell sick while visiting his maternal grandparents during a holiday.

"I visited a hospital in my mother's home district, escorted by my aunt because I was having a high-grade fever. After waiting on the bench for many hours to be seen by medical personnel, a child down the queue had a seizure and died while waiting, and a few minutes later, a young woman was being carried out of the hospital's maternity ward by a group of men after she had died in childbirth. She was followed by wailing relatives, many of them women."

"Go on, what happened next?" Jay encouraged him to continue with the story.

"That day we did not see a doctor, we were told as the day was nearing the end that he was very busy, and we must return. People, especially mothers, started to pick up their children, put them on their backs and headed out of the hospital gate, empty-handed and my Aunt and I followed the rest and headed home. I wondered aloud as we travelled back home, alternating between walking a few meters and being carried on my aunt's back, why the child couldn't get the medicine and why a woman would die while giving birth, a question I do not remember her answering. I made a resolution that day, that I would grow up and study to be a doctor so that people like the small child who died in the line, the woman who died while giving birth, or even myself, who waited the whole day in vain to see a doctor, would be taken care of. I would work hard to make sure people saw a doctor, and women did not die in childbirth."

"Hmmm, that's not bad at all," Uncle Jay responded.

"I also realized that I wanted to be a Lawyer to defend people against injustice, but I think that as a Doctor I will be able to save lives," Maanzi concluded.

"That is very good. Look at us, two starving souls, with no food to eat, unable to save our own lives from hunger and yet dreaming of saving lives," Jay said with a chuckle.

"Are you laughing at me?" asked Maanzi with a dry mouth.

"No, I was not laughing at your dreams, I was just imagining how good it would be if one day you become a doctor."

"And if the doctor does not work out, I could become a pilot, you know. What do you think?" Maanzi looked up at his Uncle as he asked, maybe expecting a loud laughter this time around. But Jay's face was now serious.

"Okay," Jay said and then silence again as both men used their last energy and begged their legs to at least give them a few more hours before they would be able to get home and have some home-cooked meal from Mary.

After a few minutes, Jay broke the silence again, maybe as a distraction for their aching legs.

"Do you know anyone in your family who is at least a nurse?" Uncle Jay asked.

Was that a trick question? Because they were related, Maanzi knew that Uncle Jay knew they did not have any such relatives. Not at the time, and not to his knowledge.

"No," Maanzi replied with a puzzled look on his face.

"A teacher, a doctor, a political leader?" Uncle Jay continued.

"No, you are the only teacher that I know," Maanzi answered.

"Not a teacher yet, I am a college student studying to be a teacher," Uncle Jay corrected him.

"So, what makes you think that you can become a doctor then?"

As if reading from a script, Maanzi replied, "Because I will work hard, I will be good to people, I will be disciplined, and I will sacrifice for it to come to pass."

Uncle Jay had emphasized these qualities; it was second nature for Maanzi to respond.

With a grin on his face, "If we can go without food and still get good grades in class, then it can be done," said Uncle Jay.

And there was silence again, and both this man and the boy begged their legs to keep going a little more, even when their strength was all gone, but looking forward to a real meal in many days or even weeks. Indeed, the meal they had that night was a feast. Maanzi ate so much that he was not able to sleep well because of stomach-aches from overstretching.

Mary was happy to see her husband. Kemi was growing and now could talk. She was shy and could not get her eyes off her father that she had not seen in three months or so. The next day, the holiday chores would start. Gardening, looking after goats, fetching water, gathering firewood and tending the few cows that Uncle Jay's father owned for the family.

As it was their ritual, when the school time was nearing the beginning, Jay moved around the village looking to borrow a bicycle to take some bananas to sell in the town away from their home and to load their belongings on. They carried their mattress, suitcase to and from the school. Both Maanzi and Uncle Jay shared a mattress, which they placed on the floor of their schoolhouse. Uncle Jay had a bed whenever they went home for holiday, but Maanzi still slept on a mat on the floorhe took a holiday from the mattress.

One day, when school was in session, they walked back to their schoolhouse at lunch, wondering what they would eat, Maanzi and

Uncle Jay found fresh food at their house in front of the door. Someone unknown to them had left it for them there. The joy they had from that gift was immeasurable. Uncle Jay tried to suppress a smile, but Maanzi did not care what anyone thought, simply grateful that they would have food to eat for a while yet.

"Maanzi, quick light the fire, and I will peel the matoke. See, we have food for lunch."

Eventually, this was repeated; it usually came from one of the other students' parents, the two came to learn later. Maanzi wondered if they were given food because both he and his uncle looked malnourished and he could not prevent his tummy from grumbling in the afternoon classes or were the parents simply being good to them? Whatever their reasons were, Maanzi was grateful for each bowl of beans or bag of potatoes as they knelt to give thanks.

Prayer was very important to Uncle Jay and his family. His father had been a charismatic Christian who woke everyone up at five o'clock to pray, and in the evening, after supper, just before bed, again he summoned everyone to pray. His prayers would usually span hours. Maanzi could remember some holidays when he would fall asleep during prayers and wake up just in time to say the long-awaited "amen" at the end.

Soon Uncle Jay shared with one of his tutors how he was getting to a breaking point. Fate had it that this tutor's family lived near the primary school where Maanzi and Uncle Jay lived. He spoke to them, and they offered to take care of Maanzi over the weekends. Maanzi could not believe his good fortune and the goodwill of this family. He would, therefore, do his homework on Friday evening and wake up Saturday morning to find that Uncle Jay had already gone to the college. Maanzi would then walk to the tutor's home.

This new family had other children as well. Once Maanzi arrived, he would join them as they went to their gardens to dig. He surprised members of his host family when he displayed his skill and speed at gardening. This family also graciously decided to give fresh food to Uncle Jay, whether Maanzi helped in the gardens or not, and this soon ended the bout of starvation that the two had endured. But in the little boy's mind, the questions lingered.

The hard work began to pay off. Maanzi began to excel in school, and Uncle Jay could not be happier.

Bursting with pride after Maanzi got another excellent report card, Uncle Jay said, "A child does not have to become what his parents are but can learn and become better. You are now on your way to changing your life; keep working hard."

"I will," said Maanzi.

Maanzi began to believe that it was possible to achieve his dreams, but he also knew that these dreams would not come easily. Uncle Jay was living proof of that.

He thought about his mother and his cousin Zuri more often and missed them deeply.

"I will see Zuri soon I hope," he thought to himself.

Chapter 9

ONE HOLIDAY, MAANZI, AFTER FAILING TO GET PERMISSION FROM Uncle Jay to go back and visit his family, whom he had not seen since he left home, decided to take matters in his own hands. So, one Friday evening, after returning from fetching water, he realized that Aunt Mary had gone to visit the neighbours and taken Kemi with her. He seized the opportunity, escaped and walked home to visit his family arriving at dusk. He arrived home as his parents and siblings were getting ready to go to bed. His mother was excited to see him and gladly embraced him. His father, however, was suspicious, and even before he greeted him, he asked, "Did you get permission to come and visit?"

Maanzi remained silent, head bowed in shame as his father glared at him with a look that said, "I thought so."

"You may stay for the night," his father said sternly. "However, tomorrow, you will go back to Uncle Jay. Look to it that it is the first thing you do after waking up."

Maanzi nodded, happy that he was not sent back in the middle of the night. His younger sister, Mercy, was already tugging on his pants, demanding attention and requesting that he tell her stories about the places he had been to.

"Aaanzi, Aaanzi," Mercy said, using the name she called her brother.

"Where have you been? What is your school called?" she continued. "Please tell me a story … please."

"I do not have any stories," Maanzi replied.

"You seem withdrawn and unhappy," Grace commented.

"No, I am fine, Mum. Just tired," Maanzi replied.

As they sat down to eat that night, all sharing food from the same round metallic platter, Maanzi had flashbacks of the many days he and Uncle Jay slept on empty stomachs, and he was grateful for that night's meal from his mother's kitchen.

Early the next morning, the only thing on Maanzi's agenda was to look for Zuri. He could not contain his excitement as he raced through their compound to the door of their house. "Hello? Zuri?" he shouted impatiently, waiting for her to show up.

"Maanzi, is that really you?" she answered from inside the house. A now shy Zuri slowly walked out to meet him. She was taller than he remembered, definitely taller than he was, and beautiful.

"Hello, Zuri," he said, smiling as he reached to hug her.

As they had done so many times before, they headed out toward the banana plantation, so they could catch up. They talked about the old times, and he talked about the many schools he had been to. However, she did not say much about her school experiences, which puzzled him. Wasn't she interested in school anymore? They were so close to the end. What had happened? *Something was not right, Maanzi thought to himself.*

To encourage her, Maanzi mentioned exciting things that happened at his school, hoping these stories would cheer her up. He told her how his grades were improving when previously, he was the one who didn't care as much about school as she did. He told her how he was always working, reading, and learning under the watchful eye of Uncle Jay.

"Uncle Jay can be such a slave master, but now I enjoy it, as I am beginning to get good grades," Maanzi said excitedly. "Zuri, I will become a doctor, and you, you will be a teacher. We will be able to leave our village and move to the big city." We will change our lives. We will change our parents' lives … and our siblings, eh?" Maanzi said with passion.

Zuri remained quiet and did not show equal enthusiasm as she did in the past about school.

He had known there was something wrong the moment he realized that she didn't have any stories to tell about her school. But when Zuri remained silent after his excited talk, it finally began to sink in that something more sinister was going on.

Maanzi turned around and really observed his cousin. The look in her eyes reminded him of the way he felt when they went days on without food and when he cried all day while Uncle Jay went to college. She was in despair and had such a look of regret that she didn't need to tell him something was wrong; he knew something was amiss. But Zuri was not willing to talk about it at all. *Was this what happened to girls as they became teenagers? Are they moody all the time?* he wondered to himself, not wanting to push her too much to say what was wrong with her. However, he was running out of time and needed to get back to Uncle Jay's, and he didn't have time for subtlety.

Zuri finally caved in, and it wasn't pretty.

She turned away from Maanzi, wiping her tears, narrated what had been going on.

"Things are not the same since you left," Zuri told Maanzi. "I feel like I am always swimming against the current, and no one defends me or looks to my interests. My mother took away my dolls as well."

In one angry fit, after she was found playing with her dolls instead of watching the children, her furious mother had grabbed her doll.

"Give it to me," Kesiime had demanded, and then she took the doll and threw it in the fire. "Now, go tend to your siblings."

"It was then I realized that all I care about and dream about is nothing. No one is concerned about whether I go to school or not. So what is the point?" Zuri cried.

"Even Scola, our aunt, was removed from school last year and forced to be married. They paid twenty head of cattle, and Uncle Sam, her brother, has already used them to get himself a young bride. Imagine that. She was taken out of school and married off simply because her younger brother needed the cows to get a new wife. Now tell me, how is there still hope for me? How?"

After that, Zuri's words came like a gush, as though for a while now she had waited for an opportunity to tell someone what was on her mind, and now that it was here, she was determined to say it all. She told Maanzi that while he was blissfully tucked away at his uncle's place, she had observed her newly married aunts suffer. Some of their husbands had no regard for their wives and considered them possessions since they had paid a dowry.

"If we have no education or qualifications to help us earn a living independently, how do we hope to escape this custom?" she asked rhetorically.

"My biggest fear is that I will end up like my mother, with my identity being tied to my children and husband. I want to be my person. That's why regardless of whether my brothers are ahead of me at school and I have been in the same class for the last four years, I still go to school unashamed, even when the other children laugh at me and call me stupid."

At this, she turned and fixed her gaze on Maanzi, as though this was the most important thing she would say. Her eyes were watering as she added, "I have to finish school. That's the only way I will break this cycle." My life depends on it. I will do whatever it takes to get an education.

"You see, my life will soon end. I told you not to go and leave me here alone," she cried.

Maanzi was very silent and did not have words to say, but suddenly had a tightness in his chest as if he were having a mini-heart attack. His emotions were welling up and he was about to cry when a loud voice sounded urgent.

"Maanzi!!!!" shouted his mother.

"Where are you? You need to be going right now!" she demanded.

"I have to go now. I am going back to Uncle Jay's home. Bye. I will come back and see you. Zuri looked away and did not respond.

Maanzi said his goodbyes to his mother and siblings and headed out. His father was out on the farm looking after the gardens.

Maanzi had tears in his eyes as he headed toward his mother.

"Life is not fair, just because she is a girl?" he thought to himself.

Maanzi left Zuri, believing she would be okay. She had the determination, and she had promised that she would work hard. She would give school her best. Zuri, however, knew that of late, she had been missing school more often than before. She did not tell Maanzi that there was a talk around the home that since she would soon be of marriage age, her parents saw no reason for investing in her school fees. She was a girl and had been lucky to study more than most in the village. Now she needed to concentrate on learning how to look after a family.

Despite the school fees woes, the house chores, and having to help with her siblings, she continued to do well in their former primary school; her mid-term marks were well above average. However, she repeatedly missed the promotional end-of-term exams, for a variety of reasons. Sometimes, it was because her parents had not paid her school fees; other times, it was simply because her mother needed her to help with a newborn baby, in which case her father did not see the need to pay school fees for that particular term since she was needed at home. However, Zuri's younger brothers went to school; one of them was in the same class as her, and two were ahead of her. This situation, though discouraging, did not deter her from dreaming of becoming a teacher.

After Maanzi's visit to his cousin, one night at supper, Zuri's mother, Kesiime announced to Jackson, "The children were sent home for school fees today."

"All of them?" Jackson asked.

"What do you mean, all of them? Did you pay some fees and forgot?" she teased.

"Well, we do not have enough money for all of them," Jackson replied.

"We should pay for the oldest first," Zuri's mother suggested, "so that she does not miss her classes and exams."

"No, we cannot pay for Zuri," her father replied.

"Her fee is so much, it could pay for the three boys." Jackson reasoned out aloud.

Zuri did not appreciate that her brothers were constantly favoured over her. Her school fee was paid last; she was told to do the household chores without their help, as that would distract them from studying, and if her parents needed someone to stay away from school to help them, it never was one of the boys.

Maanzi ran nonstop from his parents' house to Uncle Jay's home, a distance of close to ten kilometres.

"I see a dead man walking," Kemi told Maanzi upon his arrival.

As he entered the house, he had mixed feelings. He was afraid because he knew that he would be severely punished for the stunt he had pulled. He didn't care, though, because seeing his family and Zuri was worth the punishment. However, he was also angry that he would be punished for simply going to visit his family. Fortunately, Uncle Jay was not around when he arrived. However, when evening arrived, Jay returned and was like a man possessed.

"Come here and tell me why you escaped yesterday without telling us where you were going," Jay demanded.

Maanzi, tears rolling down his face already, had no answers. He was more worried about his torn pair of old pants that he had on, that he would feel the lashes directly on his bottom, and he did. He does not remember how many because he switched off his mind and tightened his buttock muscles to lessen the perception of pain.

"You know the rules," Jay said. You cannot simply go in and out as you please.

He beat Maanzi severely to erase all thoughts of ever planning to escape again, and it did work, as he still had trouble walking for a few days after the punishment.

Chapter 10

IT WAS THE BEGINNING OF THE LAST TERM OF THE YEAR FOR both Uncle Jay and Maanzi. In the coming year, Maanzi would be in Primary 6, while Uncle Jay would finally be finishing college and sit his final exams. As Aunt Mary prepared millet grain flour, maize flour, and ground nuts for the two to take, Uncle Jay went about borrowing a bicycle. Their usual routine. After a couple of rejections, he was able to secure one.

They loaded the bicycle with the mattress, the suitcase, and food stuffs to last them as long as possible. They began their usual trek to the school more than forty kilometres away. It was early morning, planned in such a way that Uncle Jay would be able to return the borrowed bicycle and if possible, make the journey back. But if it was very late, Maanzi could now stay with Jay's Tutor's family that had graciously allowed to stay with him on the weekends when his uncle went to college.

On their way back to school, Maanzi noticed Uncle Jay was unusually nervous. He kept talking about all kinds of things, laughing and using the bicycle horn to greet everyone who passed by. This was strange behaviour for the usually sombre man.

He is a teacher. Why is he worried about his exams? Maanzi thought to himself.

Jay was only a college student, however; he had been allowed to teach through an arrangement with the primary schools where they lived to help raise his tuition. He usually taught the class that young Maanzi was in, so naturally, he was his "teacher"; that's all his young apprentice knew.

Their term was going as routine. Jay would teach Monday to Friday, and then walk to college on Saturday and Sunday and back. They continued to struggle with affording enough food most of the time, but they had learned how to survive.

Then, one Sunday evening toward the end of the academic year, Uncle Jay returned with great news:

"I am not going to be walking to the college on the weekend ever again," he announced, handing over a rolled certificate to Maanzi.

"Here, look at it," he said. "That is what we've been struggling for. Finally, it's done. I passed my exams!"

That was a great cause for celebration, and Uncle Jay spared no expense. He went to the butcher's and bought half a kilo of meat and half a kilo of rice, which they cooked and ate, both greatly anticipating better days to come. There were no phones, so he could not call his wife. There were no postal addresses, so they could not write a letter. His wife and family would have to wait until the primary school closed and they visited for holidays to hear of this great news.

However, the future remained uncertain for Maanzi, and he voiced these concerns as they ate. "Where are we going to be living next?" he asked.

Uncle Jay smiled and replied, "We will be living at home with your aunt Mary and cousin Kemi. I will be teaching at that school near my home. We do not have to walk a long distance again. We will not be begging for a bicycle to transport us back here anymore. But best of all, at least we will always have food straight from our garden, which means no more starvation."

Maanzi did not respond, instead, he continued to enjoy the meat and rice, a treat indeed.

"Do you remember the week we spent eating one avocado a day each and by the end, we were all sick?" Jay asked Maanzi.

"Yeah, I remember it like it was yesterday. You were not able to go to college that weekend because you were too weak to move," Maanzi said.

The two managed to laugh, but suddenly Jay had a look of sadness in his eyes.

"Uncle Jay, what is it?" Maanzi asked.

"Nothing. I am just so happy. I hope you find that our sacrifice was worth it and that you have learned to keep fighting despite the odds," Jay said as he looked away, tears in his eyes. It was one of the times Maanzi had seen him being emotional.

Maanzi was excited for his uncle, ecstatic. But he wouldn't help the lingering sad feeling. Moving would mean losing his friends, as he would have to start a new school again. They had been at their current school for two years. This was the longest they had been anywhere, and it was the first time he could remember making meaningful relationships with his classmates. Also, the move would mean more household chores and less time to study. But Maanzi was determined to study and work hard, just like his uncle, whatever it took.

He looked up just in time to hear his uncle say, "This is just the beginning of great things."

"I will start by buying a bicycle when I start to work." *I can't wait*, Jay said to himself.

Chapter 11

JOY FLOODED UNCLE JAY'S HOME FOR A WHILE AFTER THAT. THEY had left the schoolhouse and were now living at Jay's home. More often than not, you could hear Uncle Jay's laughter as he visited with someone; the roar almost shook the walls of their house. You could hear him hum all sorts of hymns as he went about his business, but "Great Is Thy Faithfulness" was now his favourite.

Aunty Mary, his wife, and Maanzi's two young cousins, Kemi and Jacob, who were now aged five and two but had barely known their father before, would more often than not be found next to him. Kemi especially clung to him and demanded his attention, as she sang and danced for him. The proud father, of course, was happy to give her an audience.

Indeed, these were good times. Uncle Jay's joy was only compounded after a few months when he brought home his very own bicycle. Granted it was not new; it had previously belonged to Mr. Kamugisha, the local butcher, who had wanted to sell it, as he had fallen

onto hard times. Uncle Jay had saved his salary and then sold some bunches of bananas in the nearby town to come up with the money. It cost him an equivalent of $20 (50,000 Uganda shillings). He had to bargain so that the price was reduced again and again, and then that was it: his very own bicycle. Indeed, these were good times. No more humiliation as he went from house to house, begging for a bicycle. This was it.

Maanzi had felt a little out of step after they moved back home. Where previously he had had his uncle's undivided attention, Uncle Jay's time now was shared with the rest of the family, and he felt a little left out. Since there were two children now, Maanzi had more chores to do, so he focused on that in an attempt to take his mind off things. But still, he missed his uncle and the time they spent together as he watched the happy family, eyes with longing as Uncle Jay tickled the little Jacob while he washed the dishes.

However, the bicycle changed that. Until this time, Maanzi had not learned how to ride a bike, because Uncle Jay would not allow him to practice on a borrowed bicycle. They could not afford to see anything happen to a borrowed bike. However, with his new prized possession, much as he did not want anyone else to ride it, it was out of necessity that he had to teach Maanzi how to ride. Uncle Jay needed his help during the harvest season, so this was a good motivation for Maanzi.

So, it was. The two would spare a few minutes in the evening a few days a week so that Uncle Jay could teach Maanzi how to ride. On the weekends, Maanzi helped his uncle to push the bicycle loaded with farm produce through the muddied trails to the seasoned roads.

Uncle Jay, a very frugal but honest man, would return from these sales in the evenings, having spent the whole day with little to no food, afraid of buying food and reducing his savings. Then he would tell his wife how much he had made, proud of his accomplishments.

Mary was in charge of keeping the savings. Jay did not have a bank account. Uncle Jay and Aunt Mary had a relationship that was not common in these parts. Aunt Mary voiced her opinion, but more importantly, Uncle Jay listened to his wife and was open to her. In a culture where women were considered possessions, the kindness this man and his wife displayed to each other was a thing to behold.

School was difficult, as always. This was to be his final year in primary school. It was a new school, and Uncle Jay was once again teaching his class. Maanzi was to sit national exams at the end of that year, and Uncle Jay had set a high standard for him. Since Uncle Jay taught his class, he frequently picked Maanzi out to answer questions, and if he didn't know the answers, he was punished.

"You should know better," Uncle Jay would say to him in explanation of why he was being punished. "You could have asked me at home to help you with this."

Maanzi was frustrated, though he would never dare voice his concerns. Granted, he didn't study as hard as he could have, but there were valid reasons why. There was less time for completing homework because of all the added chores, and since Aunty Mary was expecting a third child, she was tired most of the time.

So Maanzi took on the roles of peeling bananas, fetching water, cooking the meals to help Aunt Mary. This left no time for him to study. Besides, Uncle Jay himself was preoccupied with his family.

Maanzi sat in his seat, head down, eyes with unshed tears. He was failing his uncle and could not see a way out of it, but he would try harder, he resolved to himself, work faster, and hopefully, he would have more time to study. Or maybe he would stay at school a little later and complete his homework before he went home. Whatever the case, he would give it his best shot.

As he was agonizing over what he would do, he soon discovered two brilliant brothers in his class. These two had been heading their class since primary one. One of the brothers was named Favour; he came up to Maanzi and offered tips on how to survive the discipline in this new school. He told him that he could not handle the new school if he resorted to tears every time he had to be disciplined.

"Leave the crying to the girls," Favour advised.

"Teachers will keep picking on you if they see that you easily cry."

By the end of his first term in this new school, the three became friends and started to compete for the top position in the class.

Even when he was weary at the end of the day, he pushed himself further. Favour, his brother Tom, and Maanzi were alternately the best in class for the subsequent terms and took pride in their position.

"What do you want to become when you grow up?" Favour asked Maanzi.

"I want to become a doctor. I want to be able to treat people and save lives."

My brother and I want to become Engineers. And make cars and all that. Favour reported with a rare confidence.

"Those are big dreams," Maanzi replied.

"Yes, I know. We already have a workshop and have made our first car," Favour told his friend. "You should come by and see it. It will blow your mind away."

Soon they invited Maanzi to their workshop. It was a small area at the edge of their compound, far away enough for their mother not to tidy things up. Here they had all sorts of metal scraps, broken tires, and planks of wood. Their current invention was a wooden car: a simple rectangle made of wood that could seat four children. At the base were four worn bicycle tires. The two brothers had gotten them from a junkyard near their home trading center, where bicycle mechanics worked. A wooden stick thrust into the tire spokes acted as the brakes. They spent their days touring the village in the simple gadget whenever they could; when they were on flat ground, one of them would push the gadget to get it in motion. And when they got onto a downward slope, they all jumped into the 'car' and rolled downhill.

The three studied together and prepared for the final national end of primary seven exams called primary leaving examination (P.L.E). Maanzi had been in this school for only two years but felt that he made great friends in the brothers.

As primary school came to a close, Maanzi was a little sad. Again, he had made great friends; he had settled into the new way of life, but now the future was uncertain. Uncle Jay had done his part and ensured that he had completed primary school. Now he had to return to his parents, who would have to pay for secondary school. Would they have the money? They had had more children while he was gone. Where would the money come from? How was Zuri faring? Was she able to continue with school? God, he hoped so. It had been four years since he had been away from home, and it had changed him. It had made him more independent. Would he fit in with everyone else? So as the national exams came closer, he moved to a bigger school, yet another new primary school where the exams were going to be conducted. His previous school had no formal registration with the ministry of education to conduct national exams.

Once the final exam was done, he packed yet again and began his trek back to his parents' home. It was the end of primary school. It had been a long journey but a journey he was glad to have taken. He had later learned that his parents did not want him to return home during the primary school years he spent with Uncle Jay, partly, to protect him from 'homesickness'—the parents worried that if he visited his home, he would perhaps want to stay home, in his familiar surroundings and refuse to go back or worse still, he could have learned of their struggles and they were not sure how he would emotionally and mentally react to the situation but most important, how this could affect his progress and performance in school. The solution was to keep him away from home.

Uncle Jay had something to say as he bid him farewell, "I will not accept anything less from you. You have seen me work hard, so you must do the same."

Uncle Jay had wanted to keep him and find a way of supporting him with secondary school as well. But his family dynamics had now changed, he had children of his own and was taking them through school. The decision was made, Maanzi would return to his home. Jay had done his part. He had, in a practical way demonstrated to Maanzi, that one can change their lives through education. But the challenge was how he would afford the education, and whether his parents would afford now that it would cost more than when he was in lower primary school. His parents had troubles affording fees before, and now there were even more children, with no stable income.

Chapter 12

MAANZI SHOULD NOT HAVE WORRIED AS HE WENT BACK HOME TO his parents and siblings. Sure, there were things that he took a while to get used to. Being the eldest, his younger siblings looked up to him and would follow him around wherever he went; there were six children now, where there had previously been four. His younger siblings hung onto every word he said and took what he said as gospel truth. This was a bit disconcerting and took some getting used to. He simply wanted to fit in with everyone, but somehow, he was the special child. He felt like a visitor in his own home.

He received his results for the national primary exam: He had aced them. He hoped that Favour and his brother Tom had aced theirs as well. However, this new scenario seemed to place him ahead of his siblings, and he was used as an example throughout their homestead. Children were encouraged to study hard and be like him. However, some adults sneered and asked what good this education was, as his father was still very poor.

"We hear that Maanzi passed his exams," villagers would be heard whispering.

"What good is that? He couldn't go anywhere. His father can't afford fees," one villager responded.

Fortunately, even with all her troubles, Zuri still treated him the same. When he came home, he discovered that she was two years behind because of all the problems she encountered. However, during that holiday, they spent every day together, just like the old times; they even tried to do their chores together.

One afternoon, just before the busy evening rush to prepare food started, they sat in their mutual compound, leaning against the walls of Zuri's house as they pondered the complexities of life.

"Remember how we used to fake falling sick in order not to go to school?" Zuri asked,

"Uh-huh, hmm, how could I forget?" Maanzi replied.

"I would give anything to stay in school now, anything!" Zuri said.

"My parents are complaining about my declining grades. It's the same old story. They complain that it's a waste of money, and worse still, I heard my mother say some time ago that I should at least finish primary school, then I can help her with the house chores full time, after which they hope I will be able to get married. I don't think I'll be able to go to secondary school."

Maanzi was silent, feeling out of depth on what to do or say to encourage her but hoping she would derive comfort from the fact that he was there, listening to her.

"I do not want to get married," Zuri cried. "I want to study and become a teacher. I want to go and live in a city, be able to buy myself a beautiful blue dress, travel places, and see how other people live. But I worry that may not be in the cards for me."

She paused, close to tears. Slowly, she was beginning to accept that she may not attain her dreams. This frustrated her to no end. She had done her best, and even then, it was not good enough. As they both gazed at the horizon, in the distance, looking but not quite seeing anything, an elderly man with a bamboo cane passed by. They saw him, but somehow it did not register that he had passed. Their little minds were fixated on the injustices of the world and their own inability to change them.

They were both startled back to reality when they heard a familiar voice from inside the house.

"Zuri? Where are you?" her mother called.

She kept calling until she opened the door to find them both seated outside.

"Why didn't you respond when I called you?" she asked. "Anyway, your siblings are crying, and I need your help."

Maanzi said good-bye and rushed back home as Zuri turned to enter the house with her mother. There would be many times that the same conversation was repeated between the two. Zuri needed to vent, as though by recounting her situation, it would get rid of her desire to pursue her studies further. As though if her parents overheard their conversation, they would realize how badly she wanted to finish school and how they were wrong to deny her what they so willingly gave to her brothers. Whatever the reasons, over and over again, Zuri vented and Maanzi listened.

Maanzi was also having problems of his own. He had worked hard and excelled at the national level exams, and while he hoped to proceed to secondary school, he soon realized that he had to overcome some hurdles first.

One evening, when he had already been accepted for secondary school, in one of a relatively modest schools, but one that would require more money than his parents could afford, Maanzi had more faith than ideas.

His father dropped the bombshell, after exhausting all his ideas on how to get enough money to send his first-born son to school.

"I think you should redo your final year of primary school," his father, Francis said.

They were sitting by the fire, having supper. His other siblings had been arguing about who was taking more food. Schools were about to open; however, Maanzi still had no idea when he would be going. Very few of his lucky friends in the neighbourhood had already completed their admission forms for secondary school and were excited, especially those who were going to boarding school. Maanzi, on the other hand, had yet to hear a word from his father. After stressing for a few days, he decided to broach the subject at dinner. He was disappointed to hear that his parents were hoping that he would repeat his final year.

He was speechless for a minute as he stared at his father, mouth wide open, wondering whether or not he was serious. But from his expression, Francis truly meant what he was saying.

"But Dad, I was even accepted in the school that was my first choice," Maanzi began, unwilling to believe that his dreams could so easily slip away. This could not be happening. He had worked hard and given it his all. But somehow, still that was not enough.

"Why?" This time, he dared to be defiant. There was a lot at stake.

"Why should I redo a class that I have worked hard to pass?" he asked.

His appetite fled from him immediately and could not eat anymore. He was too upset to do anything.

"Because Uncle Jay and I think that you could do better than you did this time and, who knows, apply for a much better school next year and aim higher," his father replied.

Better schools cost more money, money that they didn't have and probably would still not have in the years ahead. No, this wasn't about better grades; it was more about buying time.

"I don't want a better school, and I don't want to repeat a class," Maanzi's replied angrily.

"Look, you are just twelve years old; you are very young, younger than most people are when they start secondary school. Repeating a year would not affect you much. You would still be with your age-mates in the same class," Francis justified.

At that, Maanzi withdrew. His father's mind seemed made up, and that was a very difficult thing to change once he had decided on something. Maanzi was frustrated to no end. But worse still, he felt helpless. Would he end up like everyone else around him? Would that be his life? Francis had mentioned that even Uncle Jay had agreed with his proposition that Maanzi should repeat a year in primary school. Was that true?

Uncle Jay knew better. He knew how to sacrifice to get an education. Could it be possible that he would join forces with his father to prevent his progress? Somehow, Maanzi did not think so. Maybe he should ask his mother to plead with Francis. He usually got a positive response from her, more often than his father.

The next day, after his father took the few cows to graze in the pasture, he followed his mother into the garden, claiming he needed to help her. Surprised but pleased, Grace had agreed to take him.

It was early morning, and the weather was nice. The sun was just right. Not too hot, neither too cold. Today, Maanzi and his mother would be clearing the bush on a piece of property that had been let to lie fallow, in preparation for planting when the rains would come. He had broached the subject as he dug, avoiding eye contact, and she was dismayed. She ceased to dig, knowing that this was more important.

Looking straight at her son, with a determined and stern face, his mother responded;

"Your father and I do not have enough money to send you to that secondary school," she blurted out. "Perhaps we would have saved some for you by next year."

At least she was honest. She didn't play him for a fool. But that didn't help his agenda. Besides, they both knew that he would be going to secondary school when he was in his final year in primary school. How come they were not able to save then?

"Mum, please," Maanzi pleaded with unshed tears in his eyes. "You do not really appreciate what I went through to obtain these grades. I had to live away from home, as if I did not have parents." That was a low blow, and he knew it even before the words came out.

His mother, stung by the statement, replied, "I was there when you left. You think it was easy for us? You were too young to know this, but at the time you left, your father could barely afford your school uniform, let alone your tuition fees. Uncle Jay was our only hope, and he did us a great service."

"But there are no guarantees. What if I fail the exams this year, then what happens?" Maanzi insisted. He knew he was pushing hard, but she was his only hope.

"You still don't get it. The school that was your first choice is too pricey, and we hope that we'll have saved enough by the next year. We are not calling it quits, just telling you to wait."

But Maanzi insisted, "I gave it my best shot. I don't think I can study that hard again to achieve something I already have achieved. There's no point!"

His mother stared at him, caught between her son's very sensible dreams and their dire financial situation. There was no "Uncle Jay" to help further her son's dreams this time, and with the other children, there was only so much they would do. She was silent for a while. She stared at the hills beyond them. Then she turned to him and asked, "What if we enrolled you in a secondary school that is not as expensive as your first choice?"

Maanzi could not believe what he was hearing.

"It won't be as good as the first one, but at least you get to move on," she continued.

Knowing that this was his only choice and deeply grateful, he quickly replied, "Of course. I'll go anywhere! It doesn't matter. Just please don't send me back to primary school."

He was ecstatic at the prospect of moving to secondary school, regardless of where this would be. He jumped up and hugged his mother, and she was glad.

"I promise you, I will give it my best. I will not let you down," he said.

She simply nodded, teary-eyed, as she went about her business. It was the right decision.

The rest of the morning went by so fast, Maanzi every enthusiastic and digging energetically.

Chapter 13

SO, IT WAS ARRANGED THAT HE WOULD GO TO A RURAL SCHOOL that was near where his maternal grandparents lived. It was a very small school and poorly funded. It was still run under the church, having been started by parents themselves. It was expected that in secondary school, all classes should be conducted in English, but this was not always so, as some of the teachers were not fluent. The parents of most of the children were peasant farmers. The quality of a school was based on the student performance in the national exams that were written after successful completion of Form 4 and Form 6 (fourth and sixth year of secondary school); however, for this school, nobody asked how the students performed. Nobody hoped to excel, and definitely, no one aspired to go to college or university. They were here to learn about the basics, and hopefully, the few lucky ones would enroll in the trades.

The secondary school was composed of three incomplete single-story buildings that housed four classrooms, a staffroom and offices. The rooms did not have doors, but there were a few windows. There was a large compound and a football pitch at the back where the students could play, but not much else for entertainment. A little farther on, other buildings were being constructed. Dirt roads joined the buildings. There were tall mango trees in the compound whose fruit never did ripen, as it was picked by the hungry students before it could mature. The classes were crowded, with about sixty students in each room. The class had long desks that were shared by four students. There was no library, no electricity, no laboratory and no running water. The school had a few textbooks that were to be shared and read while at school and were kept on the shelf in the corner of the room that was used as a staff room. The school secretary always had the books under lock and key. No student was ever allowed to take any book home.

Most teachers, like their students, were poor and walked to and from school daily, as only a few had bicycles. School maintenance was by the students, and on occasion, they were asked to help carry stones that would be used to construct the other buildings.

It was a mix, as some students whose parents could afford more, and they were from very far distances or out of the district, resided at school. They lived in the church houses and the school had also rented out family houses of villagers around the school. Some were boarding at the school. However, most of them walked to and from home every day.

Maanzi was determined to give it his best shot. Being here was a dream come true. He was well aware that his parents, were sacrificing a lot for him to be there, and he did not take that for granted.

His parents agreed that he would stay with his grandparents during the school term, as it would be shorter for him to commute to school. However, during the holidays, every holiday, he would come home to his parents and siblings. He was also allowed to visit on the weekends if he wanted to, but the distance prohibited this. He was already walking long distances to school every day, so that the weekend, though spent on helping the grandparents with chores and looking after cows, was a good way to rest and prepare for the coming week. He did not return home unless it was necessary until the end of the term.

Chickens, goats and bananas were sold, and somehow, school fees for the first term was available. In any case, the fees to this rural small school was almost less than a tenth of what standard secondary schools were paying. It's difficult to imagine, but Maanzi's first school fees were an equivalent of 2 dollars.

This time, the good-byes were not as sad. He had school to attend, and he would see his family more often. Francis bought Maanzi a metallic box, three feet long, three feet wide, and one foot deep, that he could use to store his belongings. This box was a source of pride, as none of his other siblings had one. However, being of small stature, he could not carry the case, so Francis opted to carry it for him as they walked the long way to where the grandparents lived.

Maanzi could hardly contain his excitement at the prospect of starting school. For the first time, as long as he could remember, his tuition fees had been fully paid at the start of the term, so he did not have to worry about missing school due to unpaid school fees. Of course, there was no allowance given, but that didn't worry him. He wasn't used to having money anyway.

School started, and Maanzi had the usual hurdles to climb. He helped his grandparents with their chores every late evening and then rushed to school under the cover of the dark every morning, whether there was rain or heavy fog. On his way, he would meet other classmates who lived nearby, and together they made the daily trek to school. This was not a school in the neighbourhood. No, it was a good more than seven kilometres one way. The school provided a hearty meal of *posho* (corn flour bread) and beans every day for lunch, but he had his dinner at his grandparents' home.

After the first year, the distance was getting unbearable for Maanzi. His mother reached out to her distant relatives, who graciously accepted to stay with him because they lived near to the school, in fact just outside the fence. His parents could not afford the extra money for him to stay at school, as it were, the parents were already hanging by their teeth to raise the school fees.

At this school, classrooms had dust floors which had to be watered to keep the dust away, there was no running tap water and no electricity. Students took turns to help the potters fetch water from a stream to prepare our meals and walk many kilometres into the forests to carry firewood back to school. The school did not have a truck or any form of vehicle to help with any transportation. Most teachers walked from their homes to come to school every morning and went back to their homes in the evening as did most of the students. Very few teachers could afford to own bicycles.

For the students who resided at school, there was no library, and there were at least three(3) kerosene lamps, around which they would all crowd to catch a glimpse of light as they studied in the night. At ten in the night (10:00 pm), the lights would be put out and everyone would have to go and sleep. They would then awake at 5:00 am to read for an hour. Since Maanzi lived with his mother's relatives in the vicinity of the school, he took advantage of studying with other students in the night around the kerosene lamps.

Maanzi remembers vividly when the school acquired two(2) kerosene pressure lanterns. It was like night and day, they were very bright, and the four years were divided into two groups; the junior two years (Senior 1&2) shared one lantern while the other was for the senior two years (Senior 3&4).

The headteacher, Mr. Yacobo, was young. He was a recent graduate from a teachers' college, and he was determined to make a difference in each student's life. Yacobo was very passionate about education. This was because of his experience in trying to acquire an education. During the time when the country was at war, and the recent government was fighting the bush war, his parents had sent him to a seventh-day Adventist run teachers' college near where the guerrilla war was. He had spent so many hours or even days on the very pot-holed roads going to school. His parents, together with other leaders in their church, had started this church-run small secondary school, so they did not have to send their children across the country in search of a faith-based school. Yacobo was full of purpose, but even more than that, he was living that out in the way he talked to and admonished the students. His daily mantra at the student assembly was, "You have to work hard. If you want to change your future, work hard and do your homework."

Somehow, he believed that despite the odds his students were facing, they could excel. Often, after he reminded them that they were competing with students from the city schools for the few scholarships the government provided for higher learning, he encouraged them to believe that they were as good as everybody. They just had to work harder. He encouraged them to at least try before they gave up all hope of ever achieving what they wanted.

As the students listened, standing at ease as cadres, Yacobo would appeal to them, asking them to remember where they came from and the situations that brought them there, so that they could try and make something of themselves. While some of the students made fun of what Yacobo said, Maanzi took it to heart. Somehow, what he said resonated with him.

"Some of you know that your parents have given all they have for you to come and study," Yacobo would emphasize.

You know that they would rather buy themselves shoes, but because of you, they can't. They are eating food without salt so that you can come here and study, they are sick in their home and not getting out to get treatment because all the money has been given to you. Some hard choices have been made, and you, you have been the lucky ones—your poor parents have decided that you are worth this investment, so do not make them regret their decision…This was Yacobo's rally cry message every day as he stood in front of the students' assembly.

Maanzi would leave these assemblies more pumped than ever. *"I will not make my parents regret their sacrifice,"* he would tell himself every day.

Maanzi became fast friends with the other three students with whom he shared a desk. They would share this desk for the four years they attended that school. It was the first time he was able to keep the same friends for longer than two years, and he treasured them.

Maanzi excelled at school, year after year though it didn't come easy. He had to study hard. His parents were proud of him and were encouraged to continue supporting him, as they realized he was striving to do well.

However, his parents' support was a big sacrifice. To make ends meet, Grace started to make deep-fried banana cakes, locally known as pancakes, which Francis would peddle at the nearby trading center. This was considered a humiliating business, and their household became the talk of the village. It was rumoured that their eldest child was running them broke, and yet they had other mouths to feed. How did they hope to support the education for all their children if they went to such lengths for the eldest child? Others would laugh at Francis's face, saying he had sunk to an all-time low. Francis and his household were the joke at the local bars, as drunken men said that at least they got to enjoy their wealth and did not spend it where they could not see any returns.

When word got around that Maanzi wanted to be a doctor, then the taunting began.

"A doctor?" Hey, please tell your Doctor son that my stomach hurts so bad, I need his help," drunk men in the bars would joke at him as he moved around the small shops and bars to sell the pancakes to raise money.

Francis never said a word. He simply moved on to another open shop, "would you like to buy some pancakes for your children today" he would ask a prospective customer.

Maanzi's father was undeterred.

However, during the holidays, Maanzi helped to sell the pancakes, the roasted groundnuts, or small yellow bananas. If he thought that the people who taunted and humiliated his father would go easy on him because he was a boy, he was gravely mistaken, and it was a sad day when he learned this lesson.

One day, Maanzi had woken up at the crack of dawn to assist his mother as she made the pancakes; this was now becoming their ritual. In two hours, everything was done, and he was ready to go. The pancakes were counted one by one and placed in a large plastic container, and his mother helped him place it on his head. At a fast pace, he made his way to the trading center. It was a market day, and all the farmers would be selling their produce. So, he potentially had a lot of customers. He needed to get there fast. He is about 12 years old, but with an old soul.

Shortly after arriving at the trading center, panting and a little out of breath, with his hands aching from supporting the goods he carried on his head, one of the bicycle mechanics in the trading center yelled out to him.

"Hey, pancake boy, come over here. I want some pancakes," he said. Maanzi hastened his steps toward the mechanic's area, grateful for the customers. He was here to sell his pancakes and get money to buy books, the rest was irrelevant.

Though the mechanic was outright rude, he asked that Maanzi serve his five co-workers with pancakes, which he gladly did. He would count in his mind, "One shilling, two shillings, three shillings," as he handed these men their pancakes. Each pancake represented an income to him and a step toward being able to afford an exercise book.

After that, he stood and looked at him expectantly.

The mechanic seemed surprised. "Why are you looking at me like that?" he asked.

"I am waiting for my money," Maanzi replied. He shouldn't have to ask, and yet here he was.

"Oh, I don't have the change right now," he replied. "However, go and sell to everyone else, and by the time you are done, I should have some money to pay you."

Oh no, he wasn't going to let someone cheat him like that. The mechanic was stalling. Maanzi wanted to leave; however, since there were so many uncertainties, he didn't know whether he would still be around when he came back from selling the rest. No way. He was going to stay and insist because every shilling mattered. His schooling was at stake, so he stood his ground. He was very afraid at how this was going to unfold and was painfully humiliated that his need was so great that he could not let a man cheat him out of a few shillings.

But the mechanic was stalling, so he decided to talk instead.

"Your pancakes are actually not that bad, I can see that your father has taught you something useful for once. Do you also learn how to make pancakes at that secondary school?"

The day was wasting, and the crowds would soon be leaving. Maanzi didn't have any time for chit-chatting, but this man he was dealing with seemed not to realize that. Still, Maanzi stood his ground. He even begged the man, "Please give me my money," tears running down his face.

"Maybe we could repair your bicycle for these pancakes we have eaten." Now he resorted to blatant humiliation. "Oh, but wait, your father does not have a bicycle and cannot afford one. Did I see you two walking and carrying the metallic case as you went to school last year? I think I did."

Why Maanzi stayed, even he could not understand, as he endured one ridicule after another. His humiliation slowly gave way to anger.

"Just go. I told you to come back later," the mechanic insisted, and Maanzi did not want the other people to leave before he had sold anything. As he turned to leave with a heavy heart and tear-filled eyes, another woman in front of her shop was calling out to him, "Pancake boy, come over here." He was glad someone was calling him, so he walked toward her. The humiliation was so deep, and yet he dared not cry or even show it on his face.

"How are you, ma'am? How many do you want, ma'am?" Maanzi asked politely as he rested his bag on the bench in front of her shop.

"Five please, and here is your money," she said.

He then went his way to look for other customers, hoping that this man would still be around by the time he was done. The local market was now teeming with people, and he was selling pancake after pancake, and getting paid with no problems at all.

The pancakes were all sold by midafternoon, and he was pleased as he hastily made his way back to the mechanic, praying that the mechanic had the money, praying that he would not be humiliated, praying that all would go well.

"Sir, I have finished selling all my pancakes; is it possible to get my money?" Maanzi asked. "I want to go buy some exercise books before I go home," he added, appealing to his humanity. He was desperate to try anything to get his money back.

"What money? Do I know you?"

Of all the things the mechanic had tried, this was the winner. Denial.

"I haven't had any pancakes today. You can ask anyone here," he said, gesturing to the rest. "Surely even a doctor's examination would tell you that I am telling the truth," he added as his co-workers laughed. In fact, I have allergies to pancakes, so I could not have eaten your pancakes, there is no way.

"Oh, you examine me, I hear that you are so smart and want to be a doctor, go ahead," he taunted him.

Funny! Maanzi thought sarcastically. If he knew any biology at all, he would know that food began its digestion right in the mouth, and the pancakes would have been digested, so there weren't any tests for that yet. But he bit his tongue. Telling him that would not be helpful.

Maanzi stood there for a long time, with unshed tears, begging that he pay him back. He tried to guilt him into it. "My mother counted all the pancakes before I left, so she will know if the money I return home is less, and I will be punished."

Yes, it was true that his mother was aware; however, he would not be punished. He knew that in cases of emergency when he was desperately hungry, he ate two or three pancakes. At this, the co-workers ceased to laugh and asked the mechanic to give the boy his money so that he could go home, telling him that he had carried the joke for long enough. But he wasn't moved. Eventually, as the sun was setting, he realized that it would be dark soon and decided to leave. He would take a few steps and turn back, hoping the man would call him back. Every so often, he would imagine that he heard his name being called, and he would turn back, only to realize that he was imagining it. Eventually, as he was about to turn into the road that would lead him home, he saw the mechanic get onto his bike and ride in the opposite direction. So much for that.

"Why are some people so callous and evil?" he wondered.

It was dark by the time he got home, close to tears and vowing that he would not go back to the market the next day. Never again, in fact. He explained to his parents what he had endured. Francis, though angry, calmly responded, "He definitely should not have treated you like that. But you should ask him one more time. If he does not pay you, then leave him alone. Maybe he didn't have the money today and was embarrassed to tell you that in front of his co-workers."

"What?" Maanzi replied. Sometimes he thought his father's patience was out of this world.

"What option do we have?" Francis replied. "You need the money, so maybe if we negotiate and are forgiving toward him, he will pay."

Maanzi did not understand his father. Francis did not seem to appreciate what he had endured.

"You were not there," he said. "You cannot begin to imagine what I endured from him. No, I am not going back. I don't think I want to sell pancakes again."

He knew he was being unreasonable. But sometimes the things that people said hurt to the core.

"Sure," Francis replied. "You can give up selling the pancakes, and since there won't be any money for school fees, that will result in the end of school for you. You might as well go and beg the mechanic guy for a job and you can join them in drinking alcohol all day." That rebuke stung.

"Maanzi, let us go and make sure the calves in the kraal are safe for the night," Francis told Maanzi as he stood up from his stool in the kitchen and went outside. Maanzi followed him. The calves were fine. He just wanted to talk to him.

"Son, listen to me. The world does not owe you anything, and no one is there lacking sleep to see that you achieve an education. Not the mechanic guy. So, if you decide to let what people think of you and say to you define you, then, you will end up more like them, nothing will ever change. But that is not you.

Francis went on to tell him of the things he had experienced when he went out to the markets, and Maanzi was floored. Here he was pining over what some people had said, yet this was all for him, for his dreams and nobody else's. His father was selflessly enduring ridicule to help his ungrateful son achieve his dreams. As reality set in, Maanzi was ashamed. He had to try again, whatever it took. He resolved that once he was in a better situation, he would not look down on anyone in spite of what their occupation was. He began to get a sense that every person mattered and deserved to be treated with dignity and respect, irrespective of who they were. He imagined how his parents felt being ridiculed for sacrificing to take their son to school and said to himself. I would never accept anyone to ever be treated that way.

So Maanzi went back the next day; unfortunately, the man again claimed that he didn't know him.

"Pancake boy leave me alone. I don't owe you any money," said the mechanic and he walked away.

"I gave you my pancakes, for you and your workers and you refused to pay me. What if you ever need my help?" Maanzi asked with a stern face, of 'what is there to lose anyway'.

The mechanic who was bending down and tightening a bicycle part, shot up and looked at him, "You are funny, you know that?"

"What kind of help do you think I will need from you? I am allergic to pancakes, period. Now go away and leave me to work."

After that, Maanzi left, not even with a heavy chest, he realized that some people are just evil he did not bother him again.

With time, Maanzi was able to master the art of making pancakes and talking to people, and hence, he made profits selling pancakes. To further increase the profits, Francis decided to grow the ingredients required to make pancakes on the small piece of family land. These were simply cassava and baby bananas. However, while most people grew to respect Maanzi when they discovered his goals, occasionally someone humiliated him. Time and again, this threatened his resolve.

Some days were better, but some were as if they had been sent from hell.

It would be Zuri who would support him when he was weary. One evening, while he was feeling sorry for himself, he complained about what someone had said.

She was disappointed, but suddenly a light bulb seemed to go off. "What if I came with you?" she asked.

Maanzi stared at her, confused. "You think you can protect me?" he asked.

"No, silly. I think if I came with you, I would be able to raise money for my school fees as well. That way, my parents would not have the excuse that there is not enough money."

"The two of us can then share the ridicule from these people," she said with a grin.

"Are you crazy?" Maanzi protested.

"Why do you think that I am crazy, I am very serious," Zuri responded.

"Sure," Maanzi replied, feeling rebuked. But he was concerned. He couldn't say no to her. While the job he had was humiliating for a boy, to say the least, it was unheard of for a girl to make money that way. He wondered whether their association would bring more humiliation their way, especially for her. No, he couldn't deny her request, but he braced himself for the worst.

As it turned out, Maanzi should not have worried. Working with Zuri was a welcome change. After she got over the hurdle of convincing her parents that she would be able to come back in the evening in time to complete the important chores, she was allowed to go with Maanzi. Being away and working toward something boosted her spirits. Maybe this would help her complete her studies. For Maanzi, the men who previously ridiculed him became quiet when they saw him with a girl, and they would not bully him. These two cousins would sit next to each other in the market place as they sold their pancakes. When one needed a bathroom break, one stayed and took care of their products.

They were good partners too. On the days when Zuri sold all her pancakes before Maanzi, she would then take half of Maanzi's pancakes, put them on her basket and start selling for him. Maanzi would also do the same if he was lucky to sell off his pancakes faster than his friend. They would then find a secure place, sit down and count their money. On the days, when their mothers had instructed them to buy the exercise books, they would not contain their excitement as they headed into one of the shops to buy their brand-new books before heading home. Otherwise, they would count the money and head home and hand over the money to their mothers for safekeeping until the beginning of school. For Maanzi, such evenings were filled with so much joy and an adrenalin rush of 'I have books to return to school'.

Eventually, it seemed to catch on in the village that older children could work to supplement the parents' income that way. And a few more children started to sell pancakes in the market. It still remained a job for the poor of the villagers even then.

With the profits, Maanzi was able to buy a pair of shoes for the first time. These regular black plastic shoes were the rave of the village. The shoes were best worn in the cooler temperatures, as they would burn his little feet when it got hot. With these shoes, he was able to walk to and from school much faster and gain glances of admiration from some of his classmates.

Chapter 14

FROM THE MONEY ZURI RAISED, SHE WAS ABLE TO COMPLETE HER primary school and was now in secondary school. This school was near where her parents lived. She would walk to school daily and come home in the evening to do her chores. Because she was so busy, she didn't have time for rumours. To top it off, she was considered very beautiful by those who saw her. Because of these qualities, she soon became the talk for the male suitors in the village. There were more than five suitors at a time, with ages varying from late teens to forties. They all wanted a hard-working woman who had a little education. Not too much that she would oppose whatever they said but educated enough to understand how to count.

But Zuri was blissfully unaware of what was being said as she went about her business. Of course, she noticed that most guys became very friendly and would offer to carry her pail of water from the well. In the market, some men would whistle when she passed by. But they did this for other women as well, so she was not too flustered about it. She had school to complete. She'd been given the opportunity of a lifetime when she was allowed to go to secondary school, and she would not squander it.

It was the flattery she received from the teachers and other students at school that she was so unprepared for, and this would be her undoing. One of the teachers, James, was a particularly handsome man who spoke eloquently and made boring history lessons into something she enjoyed; he intrigued her. James had been educated in the country's main city and as such had a good command of English; he had somewhat of a British accent, which presented him as a polished and composed individual. She was particularly attentive in his class, which he soon noticed, and he encouraged the rest of the class to be like her.

At the end of the class, he would ask her to collect everyone's homework to give it to him. Eventually, this would lead to conversations about her dreams of becoming a teacher. He was impressed with her and encouraged her, saying since she was determined, she could accomplish her dreams. Over time, she opened up about how her parents did not particularly support her aspirations and how she had had to work hard and sell pancakes in order to help raise part of her school fees. He told her that he admired what she . was doing and then said he could help tutor her in the evening to help her excel.

Ecstatic, she quickly accepted, and this led to tutoring sessions at his home. When one of her close friends realized what was going on, she warned her in a hushed voice, saying, "How can you trust that man? Rumour has it he is not appropriate with young girls."

"He's helping me study," she replied.

"Any help I can get to stay in school and excel in school, I will take it. It is my last chance at changing my life," Zuri responded.

But anyone could see that there was more to it than that. She was smiling ear to ear whenever she came from his house. Yes, she was excelling in history but barely passing the other subjects.

Soon Zuri was able to buy things that the rest of the class could barely afford. She would go with her friend to the school canteen and pay for snacks for both of them, where they previously went hungry the whole day. She also bought another pair of shoes, and somehow all her tuition was being paid on time. For the first time.

"What happened?" her friend asked. "Did your parents suddenly come into money?"

"No," she replied. Silent.

"Be very careful," her friend warned. "That man is going to use you then leave you. He has that reputation."

But Zuri was in so deep; she thought he had to care about her. He gave her money for her tuition fees. He frequently singled her out as an example for the rest of the class. They shared similar dreams, and he was helping her achieve them. She was special to him. He had said so. No, he had to care about her.

Chapter 15

MAANZI WAS STUDYING HARD, AND THINGS WERE LOOKING UP. HE was in his fourth and final year in secondary school. That would be his last year at this school; he would still need to do two more years of high school before he could join university. His class aced the national exams and made history in the school as having the best performance that school had had to that date. Guess Mr. Yacobo's lessons were paying off. The school celebrated with them and gave each of them a much-needed kerosene lamp to help them study during the nights. Maanzi was among the top students who had passed with grade one. Maanzi and his friends, appeared in the newspaper that was produced in the city far from their village but in their local dialect. He would find this out later.

For Maanzi, it was again time to pack up and face another unknown academic future.

For his parents, it was yet another victory. Sacrifices that had paid off.

After Form 4, Maanzi had applied to one of the better secondary schools, in the western region of the country. He knew that in order to achieve his dream of going to university, and have a shot at studying medicine, he had to attend one of these schools and continue to make good grades. This school had a good reputation and a well-stocked library, and it employed some of the top teachers in the country. As a matter of fact, some of these teachers were involved in setting up the national end of high school (Form 6) exams. Following his performance at the Form 4 exams, he was accepted in the school. He had discussed it with his parents before he applied to the school, and they had agreed, not quite appreciating how much this would cost.

So, his parents received the news of his admission to the school with mixed feelings. They were proud that their son continued to excel. However, they were afraid that they could not afford the school fees at the new school. Worse still, they dreaded disappointing their son.

That year, the president had announced that the government would be able to subsidize the school fees for students, but they were phasing it in. They would start with removing the tuition fees for students attending primary school so that all the parents had to pay for was their children's scholastic materials, their uniforms, and food. Francis had been grateful when he heard the announcement, given that he now had four children in primary school. But he was hoping that the same would happen for secondary schools soon. It would only be two more years, and if Maanzi excelled, he could enter university on a government scholarship. Short of that, he would become a farmer like all of them, because the parents, even if they sold themselves into slavery, they would never afford to pay for a private education at college or university. This was where the rubber meets the road. Maanzi knew this, his parents knew this.

Although Maanzi had been accepted at one of the better schools in the city which was at approximately 50-60 km away from his home village, there was a reputation that another school in that city was far better equipped with a library, laboratory and great science teachers. Its students always did perform much better in sciences and were accepted into the only two medical schools in the country at the time.

Grasping at every chance he could get in order to maximize his opportunities to study medicine, Maanzi needed to get into the better school. He had got the grades. He decided to go to the school and appeal to the head teacher and ask if he could transfer his acceptance from his prospective school to the 'better one' as far as teaching and excelling at science subjects was concerned.

So, his parents tried their best to raise some transport money for him to travel to the city and talk with the Head teacher of this school. One day, he made the journey and showed up at his office with no appointment and begged his secretary to let him see the head teacher. It was very important. Maanzi does not know why, but when this woman saw a young man, bare footed, dust up to his knees, and yet determined to see the head teacher of a great school, she allowed him in after Maanzi narrated part of his story.

"knock, knock," Maanzi pounded on the door.

"Come in," came the response from inside. It was an authoritative and somewhat a cold voice, it was unlike the one of Maanzi's previous head teacher—which was vibrant and yet caring, passionate and sent out vibes of 'I do care about you'.

The head teacher was a middle-aged tall gentleman with shades of grey to his head.

His first look at Maanzi revealed a person who was startled at seeing him inside his office.

"Are you one of my students," he asked as his gaze was fixed to his desk and his mind somewhere in his farm.

"No sir, not yet," Maanzi responded and remained standing and he never offered him a seat. He thought to himself, "should I ask permission to sit down?"

But from his look and the way he communicated, he was obviously wanting to get him out of his office as soon as he could, and probably that is why he did not offer a seat.

Maanzi wasted no time. He immediately narrated his story that he had been in a poor rural school, but against odds, he had managed to pass his exams well and was hoping to join the great school and study in preparation for medical school. The head teacher looked at him and said:

"I see that you have done well, you have excellent grades, but you did not place your first choice to this school, this is a great school and only considers students who give it their first choice. Sorry, but we can not take you on."

"Please, sir, give me a chance, I really want to study from this school which has a great library, a laboratory and excellent teachers." Maanzi pleaded.

He finally told the young man, "We can consider your request, if you have good reference."

"Can you get a reference letter?" he asked.

"Yes, I can, and I will," Maanzi responded.

"Alright, come back and see me when you have one." By a wave of his hand, he dismissed Maanzi from his office.

As Maanzi turned to leave his office, he could not help but notice that his eyes were sizing him up and they rested on his bare feet. And there, in his eyes, was pity. The type which seemed to send Maanzi the message that, 'you should know that you are out of your depth young man'. He then gave a sigh as Maanzi was closing his office door.

His eyes locked with those of the secretary and Maanzi immediately told her that he will coming back with a reference letter soon.

He was very poor; his parents were poor. He knew it, but he also knew that he needed a chance to apply myself, in a school that was every well equipped. So, he could take that disapproving look and condescending words from the head teacher, it was just a small price to pay at the time for what he was looking for. He was determined to get into this school, because he had figured that it was his best shot at studying sciences and getting better grades to join University. And after all, he had an acceptance letter from a sister school already, but still he hoped to get into the best one at the time. He headed to the city, got a taxi back home. He already had in his mind whom to get the reference letter from: the prominent politician, who himself had studied at this 'great school' as the old boys liked to call it.

Maanzi would have to keep watch for him to return from the capital city on the weekend so that he could talk to him and ask for the letter which he desperately needed. Whenever the great politician came to his village over the weekend, there would be a line of people wanting to see him: some to beg for menial jobs in his ranch, others who asked for money to pay fees their children's fees, and yet others would be there for political favours. There was a person to vet those who entered his gate to have a chat with the great politician. Maanzi was not allowed to see him (he was bounced) twice, but on the third attempt, he was permitted to see him. It was his first time to come close to this important person. Granted, as children, they had danced and sang songs of praises for him during his political rallies and rejoiced when he won on several times. In fact, they sang the same songs with his name in them, even when he was not running for office. He was that influential, he was that popular, he had been around politics and power for a long time and still is. As children in their village, if they saw a car pass through the winding muddy paths, it could as well have been his. They would run towards the road shouting on top of their voices this great man's name.

"Professor, Professor, hello, hello," The children would shout.

But as they would be approaching the small road, the car would pass, dust would be in the air, that they would not tell who and how many people had been in the car. It, however would still be an eventful day and the children would return home and tell their parents that Professor's car had passed through the village road that day.

So, to finally meet this man up close, was very exciting. Given a chance, Maanzi would have told him all he knew about him and his greatness, power and influence that as children sang about him and for him. He was the only professor Maanzi had heard of as a child growing up in their whole constituency. What professor meant, was a different matter to Maanzi. He just knew that it perhaps meant a great person. And thinking about the fact that he had studied at the great school, gave him goose bumps and hope that, this 'great man' would also wish 'this poor boy', bare footed, whose peasant parents had worked so hard and sold everything they had to give him an education, would be gracious. Even more hopeful was the fact that if he told the professor of his desire to become a doctor, he would be more encouraging of his ambition and sympathising of his situation.

On the day that Maanzi finally got to see him, he had borrowed a bicycle from a neighbour and rode under the cover of the darkness and before dawn he was at his gate. But even then, there were at least five people ahead of him already waiting. They all waited patiently outside the gate, usually quiet, until when the professor woke up, had his breakfast and was then ready to start meeting his mostly uninvited guests, who would haunt him with small and big requests, but each request very personal and important to each visitor.

"Why are you here to see the Professor?" demanded the gateman in a menacing voice.

"I want to talk to him about school," Maanzi responded as gently but as firmly as he could muster. He did not want the gateman, who had the powers to prevent many from accessing the influential man to have any excuse for throwing him out of the queue.

Pointing to an open door a few meters ahead, he instructed, "when that person comes out, go straight in there and speak with the professor."

"Good morning, Professor," Maanzi beamed as he entered this one room that had a big table in front of the great professor and a nice love seat that he inclined in. There were around the room, benches for his visitors. So, it was obvious that this was not the room where he met with those who 'mattered'. Maanzi was tempted add to his greeting that "it was great to finally meet him in person". But the professor was not one to wait for his uninvited young, bare-footed guest to add another sentence or get bothered with pleasantries. After all, the young man looked like he had come to look for a job in his ranch.

"What do you want young man?" He asked without responding to the pleasant greeting. He had an expression of having been exhausted by everyone wanting something from him, everyday, all day, all weekend.

Maanzi did not waste his time, he immediately narrated his story and the reason he was there to see him.

"My name is Maanzi, he began. I would like to join the great school. I have been to the school to see the Headteacher, who advised me to come back and get a reference letter. I am hoping to get a reference letter from you, Sir, in order to secure a place at this great school." As he began to tell the great professor about his grades, he suddenly and impatiently interrupted.

"Son, who is your father?"

"My father is Mr. Francis," Maanzi responded.

"Can your father afford to pay school fees in this great school?" the professor demanded to know. Maanzi explained that his parents were determined to continue to raise money for his school fees and that, in fact, they were in the process of selling off a big portion of the little family land to raise his fees as he joined high school. He also assured him that he had also been working menial jobs to help his parents with raising his school fees and money for books and pens.

"We have so far done well," he said with a grin on his face that was meant to convey to him that they were okay and knew what we were up against.

Then, the professor began to speak. The words, that Maanzi will never forget, with a demeanor that he can still vividly see when he closes his eyes, and in a way that made him feel unwelcome, unwanted, unworthy–BUT, the words that changed his life. Those words stirred in him a resolve, yet again, that he was never going to allow to be defined by other people irrespective of who they were. That he was never going to speak to any person in his entire life in a way that made them feel like they were less than, that he would live his life to make sure that he learned and practiced communicating with people in a way that carried and portrayed grace, honesty, honor and love.

Maanzi sat there on the bench as I listened to what the great professor had to say to him. After listening for a few seconds, he realised that there was no help coming his way, but nevertheless, he was determined to get his help anyhow.

"The school you want to join is a great school. It is not a school for anyone, or everyone for that matter. Many important people have gone through that school. I do not see the purpose of giving you a reference letter, when your father can not afford to raise school fees to take you there. Go to the school that you have been accepted in. It is also a good school. I can't give you the letter. It would be of no use to you. You can go."

"Professor," as Maanzi began to protest, the professor insisted, "Go, there are other people waiting to see me outside," he condescendingly pointed to the door for Maanzi to leave.

Maanzi remained glued down on that bench.

"What are you waiting for, I told you to go," he looked at him surprised that the young man was still seated in his presence. His frustration was beginning to show.

"I am not leaving without that reference letter. I really need it," Maanzi pleaded.

The professor stretched out his hand, reached for a sticky pad. A purple bundle of sticky pads and wrote on top of one piece these words, "This young man would like to join the great school." and then signed his initials.

He peeled it off the bundle and handed it over to Maanzi. This got him out of his room. The young man opened a book which had his results in and tucked this piece of sticky note inside these pages protecting it from any harm. He got out, and immediately headed home. He told his parents that, after a long struggle, he managed to get a few words from the professor and would like to return to the city as soon as possible to meet the head teacher of the great school. Though the sticky note did not look anything like a reference letter he wanted, it was a writing from the great professor to his old school friend whom they had studied at this great school together. Everyone knew the professor. Maanzi was hopeful and looked forward to taking this sticky note to the head teacher and tell him that he got it from the professor himself.

When the week started, transport money had been organised and he headed to the city. When he arrived at the school, the head teacher was in fact about to leave for a major meeting. The secretary allowed him into the office immediately and reality hit him, so hard.

Maanzi opened his book, and there in the middle was the purple sticky note that he had protected from any harm. Handling it with care, he gave it to the Head teacher and told him that it was from the great professor himself. Unfortunately, at the time, there were no cell phones, so this could not be confirmed.

The Head teacher looked at the note, looked at Maanzi and with a sense of irritation told him, "this is not a reference letter."

"I can not help you. You should go to the school that has accepted you. You can now go." He was at the door, and he nudged him out of his office and left him standing in front of his secretary with tears in my eyes.

As he returned home that day, he reflected on the professor's use of his position, power and influence. The way he had interacted with him, leaving him feeling less than a human being, and what was worse was that he had been dishonest with a naïve, poor, helpless boy who was grasping on any straw to get into a great school. He had given him a 'fake' reference letter.

"Why did he do that? He basically told me and treated me in a way to let me know that my parents and myself were not worthy of getting his help, that I was not worthy of being treated with honesty and dignity and that I did not deserve a chance of studying at the great school, which he told me was not for 'everybody'," Maanzi thought to himself.

The head teacher, a friend of the professor, who had also studied at the great school and was now honored to lead it, had a similar trait of speaking and treating people likewise. Why would people that have had the greatest privilege of studying at a great school, treat other people in this manner, was his question as he headed back to his village that day.

When he told his parents, they were not surprised, and they assured him that since he was getting into a much better school than one he had attended for secondary school, all he needed was to work hard.

"Just have faith," his mother admonished. "I know you will be fine," she assured him.

The tuition fees and the school requirements are greater than what we have been struggling with, he thought. Maybe it's time to just give up. Maanzi thought to himself. He wondered how and was almost afraid to hope. But this adversity united Maanzi and his parents in a way that nothing else could have. In order to make more money, Grace woke up earlier to make more pancakes for Maanzi to sell. In addition, she took to baking bread using a charcoal kiln. She made the bread the night before, and Maanzi carried it with him to the trading center while on his pancake run. Other days, his mother gave him bananas or roasted ground nuts, anything to raise a bit of more money that could be sold from the household was put on sale.

Francis took another job working in someone's farm, taking care of his cows and clearing the bushes. The harder his parents worked, the more determined Maanzi became. The more difficult it looked to ever get out of this cycle.

During the holidays, Francis would tell his son who had not paid him for his labour and Maanzi would set out knocking on their doors asking for money "my father has sent me for his money."

"I don't have the money, come back in two days," was a common response.

And at times, "What is wrong with you people? Were you not here yesterday? I told you I don't have any money. I will tell you when I get it, bye," doors slammed! Maanzi was no stranger to collecting from those who owed him and his father, and by this time he was already a seasoned debt-collector who did not care what insults were hauled at him, he had one mission and told himself, "say whatever you want to say, all I need is for you to pay my money."

One day, Maanzi went to collect his father's wages from the farmer.

"My father has sent me for his money," he said when he arrived.

"Why does he need the money now?" the man asked. "I told him I do not have money for his pay."

"I am going back to school soon, and he has not got the fees yet. He hoped you would pay him," Maanzi replied.

"Oh, so you are the son he talks about and works hard for?" the gentleman asked sarcastically. "Tell him I do not have the money today," the gentleman replied.

"Come back tomorrow." He motioned with his hand for Maanzi to go away.

"And by the way, tell your father to come himself," the man shouted.

Maanzi returned home empty handed. His father was behind the grass-thatched kitchen sharpening his panga to head out into his own banana plantation to work for a few hours, before going somewhere for a small menial job to raise more money for Maanzi's fees.

"What did he say to you?" Francis asked with a 'hopeless' expression on his face.

"He told me that he does not have any money. That you should go back yourself tomorrow," Maanzi continued.

"That is life. Son, you see that life is not fair, you work hard, you give it all you can, for almost no money at all, but even that small wage, someone wants to cheat you out of it. Last year, he did not pay me my full wage, he claimed that I did not do a good job.

But if you look at that piece of land I cleared for his animals, it is like a professional soccer field now. We have to look for other ways of raising money," Francis concluded, sounding defeated but never in despair.

Maanzi's parents also diversified their business to include farm produce. Previously, this would not have been a good move in this particular village, because everyone grew their own food on their very tiny pieces of land; if they needed something a neighbour had, they would barter with them. Now, however, with the urbanization and towns growing near their home, they soon realized that the people in the trading centers could not grow their own food. So, this was the market they targeted.

But selling this produce was a sacrifice for the family. Given that it was predominantly a young household, Francis and Grace could only plant so much food by themselves, with little help from Maanzi and his siblings. The alternative was to sell some of the milk from the cows. When Francis announced this in front of everyone during the evening meal, they were stunned. They all knew that their local long-horned Ankole cows did not produce a lot of milk. The milk was just barely enough for the children to drink.

"I even got a customer," Francis said. "Ms. Yeza will be taking a liter of milk in the morning and in the evening."

It was awhile before Grace spoke.

"But the milk is already barely enough for the children as it is. And you are planning on reducing the little that there is?" she protested. Tears were rolling down Grace's face, for she had small children that could benefit from the little milk they were getting from their few local cows.

"Do you have any other brilliant ideas for how we can send him to high school?" he asked with a resigned expression. Grace was silent.

Maanzi had listened quietly to the conversation and then asked to leave. He couldn't take it anymore. The guilt was making him nauseous. He walked a distance in the dark and could not hold back the flood of tears. It was okay when he had to work hard, when only he and his parents were pulling the weight to further his education. But his siblings, who had previously paid for his dreams in ways that were intangible, would now feel the strain. It was painful to dream big in these parts. A person's dream was never achieved by just their own sacrifice alone; everyone who was around contributed. Everyone seemed to sacrifice, just for him, it seemed. He prayed to God for strength to study hard and prayed for health and long life to be able to pay them back and contribute to his siblings' tuition. This, like so many other things, was out of his hands.

Soon everyone adjusted. The older children and their parents started to take porridge in the morning and evenings to supplement their meals. The milk was reserved for the younger ones.

Despite the hard work and sacrifices, they still came short of what was needed to pay for even the beginning fees in high school. But by this point, with the end so close in sight, his own parents did not need any convincing.

Francis, amid ridicule and disagreements from his extended family, as a last resort decided to sell half an acre of his property. The money would hopefully be able to help his son in the high school years. So, he thought.

Very early the next morning, Francis walked to his brother's house to ask him if he would come to be a witness to the selling of his land. Jackson was outside his kitchen, sharpening his panga, getting ready to go to the farm.

Francis had shared this proposal with his family and everyone had outrightly rejected his suicide mission. They blamed him for 'blindly following his wife'. But Francis had hoped that he could convince his brother to be at the sale agreement, and if nothing else, support him emotionally.

"Why are you here, Francis?" Jackson asked. "If you think I will come to support you in your madness, then you are wrong. I will not stand by and see you sell the family land. I will not come to bear witness to it. Why are you wasting family land on one person's education? What makes you think that your son is any different from others, that he will not just waste your money and come back to ask you to sell more land?

"What is even the point of talking to you? You only listen to your wife," Jackson muttered, and he left his brother standing there.

In disbelief, Francis walked back to his compound and met the men who had come to buy his land. He signed the sale agreement, and Grace was the witness. And painfully the borders were drawn, and more than half their land was gone. They counted the money, handed it to Francis, and then Francis handed it over to Grace for safe keeping.

Maanzi was ready for the first term of high school. At a very costly price to the entire family.

There were so many uncertainties and so much had been invested, but this was the final push. And there was a lot at stake. But Maanzi was not unaware of the sacrifices. The first day of school arrived, and he packed his few clothes and shoes in the metallic case and headed to the city for the first time.

Francis, Maanzi's father escorted him to this school for his first day. This took a lot of sacrifice because extra money needed to be spent to transport two people. It was the last time he would escort him or come to see him at school for the rest of his two years of high school.

At daybreak, Maanzi and his father had trekked very many kilometers, suitcase on his father's head, small mattress on Maanzi's head, heading to the main road that lead to the city. Granted, there were a few pick-up trucks that made trips from their village to the main road, but for a fee. It was the fee that they could not afford. This journey was not a stranger to both of them. Maanzi had been trekking this path with his father when he was in secondary school. After arriving at school, school fees paid, some students helped them to locate the dormitory.

"Well, this is what we have been working hard for," Francis exclaimed.

Maanzi still feeling guilty about all the family sacrifices and with the turbulent family relationships back home because of his father selling off almost an entire piece of their family land to bring him into this school, he did not lift his eyes from the ground nor did he respond to his father.

"I hope you will not spend your time here playing. You know where you are coming from," Francis concluded. He then headed out to go get a taxi for the part of the journey, but he still had the long trek on foot for the many kilometers awaiting him. None of the two had anything to eat, they could not afford it. Maanzi made his bed and looked forward to his assured dinner.

This was a boys-only boarding school, with children from affluent families. It was the first time he was in a school in which one could participate in various sports, drama, or art activities. There were debate clubs, environmental clubs, and a Red Cross club. Local plays were brought to the school for the students to watch. There seemed to be something for everyone. The students were free to visit the town as they pleased.

The teachers were eloquent and well learned, and it was important to them that the students have a good grasp of what was taught. There were only twenty students in each class, compared to the sixty he was used to. Each person had his own desk. The school had a well-equipped library and science lab, and the road it was on was paved. The school had running water and electricity, and it had its own farm from which they would get the milk for the students and some of their food. The students would work in the farm at scheduled times. But it was mostly the students who studied agriculture who spent most of their time there. Not as workers, but as learners.

The dormitories were crowded but airy. Really, he didn't have much to complain about. From the very start, Maanzi studied like a man whose life depended on it. And it did, literally. Too many people had sacrificed to get him here for him to sit back and become distracted by the luxuries that the school provided. The family land had been sold, so he didn't have anything to fall back to. That's what he told himself every day. But really it was guilt that he should be allowed to enjoy anything while the rest of his family sacrificed for him, and a very present fear of failing the important people in his life that really drove him. Whenever he felt tired, he pushed himself for thirty more minutes.

When the teachers gave any work, he did it immediately and studied extra. On the weekends, while his friends went out of school to walk around the town, he headed to the library to study. He was a man obsessed, with unseen demons chasing him. It was too much; sometimes, one of his friends would ask, "Do you have a life outside studying? Why don't you ever go to town with us?" But he had to give school his very best shot. He thought often to himself "I would rather go back home dead than facing my parents with failure, it would kill them, they have sacrificed too much".

But even then, school was not as straightforward as he hoped it would be. Sure, he was doing his part, but Maanzi still had prejudices to overcome.

He was occasionally the joke, as he had come from a school that no one had previously heard of, nor did they know where his village was. He had a strong accent, and his English was not grammatically correct sometimes. He was small with hardly any muscle bulk, he did not know how to play soccer, neither did he watch any games. But of course, his financial situation set him apart. Since he didn't have any money to buy snacks or spend when he went to town, he was ridiculed.

Even some teachers, instead of being a source of encouragement, would humiliate him and his colleagues who had come from rural schools.

"Maanzi, which school did you come from"?

Maanzi would whisper the name.

"Where is that? Teacher would ask, drawing applause and laughter from students who had come from the more polished and recognized schools.

"And you also hope to pass and go to University to study Medicine?" once one of his teachers asked.

Maanzi didn't have any words to say to such comments. But in his heart, he would think to himself, "If you only knew how determined to succeed I am, and how desperately I need your help and how much your encouragement would mean to me, you would not say what you are saying."

Some nights as they all sat down to study, which Maanzi was grateful for because there was electricity all night. His classmates would taunt him and his fellow students who were of the low social class.

"I wonder how someone can sit and read the whole night without anything to eat. It must feel strange," one of his classmates would say.

"How do you even have a working brain without feeding it?" another would ask, laughing.

Fortunately, because Maanzi was not the only one on the receiving end of this ridicule, he became friends with Matthew, who lived in similar circumstances. He was from the same village secondary school and had been on top of their class. He was brilliant in mathematics and wanted to become an electrical engineer. The school did not provide anything to eat at break time, and the meals were only three in a day—corn flour porridge mixed with milk in the morning, corn bread at lunch with beans, and corn bread with beans at supper. Weekends were the best, because then, the corn bread was served with beef. So, every break time, as most students went on to the nearby vendors to buy some bread and tea, Maanzi and Matthew would find reasons to go back into the dormitory, or finish an assignment, or wander into the chemistry lab and work on an experiment. They became very good at organic chemistry and could change a two-carbon compound into a five-carbon compound using the longest route and multiple reactions. It was their escape from the hunger.

In order to stop the privileged students from talking about them, they would fill their empty cups with water and pretend that it was juice or milk. This did not help the situation, as laughter would sometimes break out from the back.

"Someone finally had money to buy something to eat for a change," one student called out as Maanzi and Matthew entered class holding cups.

"Yeah, right, I bet those cups are empty," yelled another student.

The two kept quiet as they moved to their desks and continued their reading.

This didn't help, but they had to try anyway.

Maanzi had very good reasons for working hard and wanting to succeed. He had left home after his father had sold their family land; they had all worked hard to afford school fees for the first term in high school and did not know if he would even make it for the next term. But against all hope, he kept thinking, Imagine, if I could get more school fees to return, what would happen if I passed my exams. Imagine the possibilities ahead.

Maanzi was now determined to do whatever it took to make it to university. He was more afraid of what would happen if he went back home and told his parents that he failed his exams, because he simply did not apply himself hard enough, than he was afraid of all the tribulations and scorn from his teachers and fellow students, who thought he would not make it because of his poor background.

He imagined what would become of his parents if he returned home and he had failed his exams. How could they ever live with such a shame, after selling all they owned and choosing to bet all of it on their son against all traditional wisdom and cultural way of doing things in their village. Imagine what would happen to his siblings if they dared dream of going to school after he had become a big disappointment.

He continued to realize that his success was really not about him but more and more about his parents and his siblings. After seeing the dedication and sacrifices of his parents, doing all they could to send him to high school, he realized how much it meant to them to provide an education for their children. He promised himself that if he made it to the university and got a job, he would dedicate his life to helping his parents educate his younger siblings. He would not allow his father and mother to continue with the humiliation of selling pancakes, nor would he want his siblings to go through that hardship, if he could afford to contribute to their education.

"We have to keep working hard and give it our best, if anyone is to come after us and succeed," Matthew told Maanzi.

Maanzi, after a deep thought, asked, "Do you think you will be able to come back next term?"

"I honestly do not know if my parents will afford school fees again," he said. "I hope that my uncle will help out, but we should not worry about next term, we have to work hard this term and do our best when we have the opportunity. Maybe we can get a scholarship."

With a wave of sadness on his face, Maanzi replied, "I want to do everything within my power to pass, and I would rather go back home in a coffin than tell my parents that I failed them. They have sacrificed so much. I do not know that my father could take the shame from the village folks." He finally put in words to a friend what he had always thought but could not say, at least not to his parents.

"We have to make it!" the two friends cried together. This was the first time they were overwhelmed to tears. Maanzi went ahead to remind his friend about his time with Uncle Jay. He narrated their story and the success of Uncle Jay.

Uncle Jay was moving forward as well.

Uncle Jay had come from begging his friends for a bicycle to buying one. He had moved from being a college student, hopping from school to school, trying to pay his way through college, to now being a teacher (even if what he was paid was so meager). He was teaching and influencing young people, and more than education, he had a platform to tell young people about life and inspire them to want to reach higher.

If anyone had reasons to work hard at school, Maanzi had them; his life depended on it, his parents' pride and dignity depended on it, and since the family land had been sold off for his school fees, his siblings' future depended on it. There was so much at stake. In the middle of the night, the flashbacks of his parents selling pancakes and his father slaving away in someone's farm to raise his school fees pained him so much and drove him to work hard and find success. He often dreamed of himself and his father working together on the neighbour's farm under the scorching sun. And whenever he could not sleep, he would spend the night studying.

He was shocking the teachers and his fellow students alike as he continued to get good grades. He was preparing for the final battle, the end of high school exams, an exam that would determine his future, and he viewed it as such. It was his only future; there was no future to go back to, not to selling pancakes, not to a family with no land, and he wanted to save his parents from the ridicule of their extended family for having sold their land to send him to school.

I will buy this land back, even more land. I will make my parents proud, Maanzi kept telling himself. There was nothing to go back to; the alternative to failing was more threatening. A life without education meant a lifetime of selling pancakes and a life without possibilities, which he had grown to detest so much.

In high school, Maanzi devised means of finding money to buy essential supplies such as tooth paste, tooth brushes, books and pens.

"Would you like me to wash your clothes for money?" he would ask fellow students.

One of the senior students, who was at the time studying for his final exam, with whom Maanzi shared a double decker bed, was gracious and would give him clothes to wash. He paid him some money, but also gave him some sugar and tea leaves when he did not have cash for his labour.

The holiday before the end of high school final term, Maanzi and a few friends decided to stay back at school for the holiday.

For Maanzi, it was two-fold; one he did not have the fees to go back home, but most important, he wanted to stay at school and use the electricity to study, day and night, without the distractions of the chores at home. This plan had been agreed to by both his parents, though, he was meant to have gone home for a few days, collect supplies in terms of food. The school did not give these few students food, but the Warden only agreed to privately leave one dormitory and one classroom open.

Maanzi's parents would try and send some matoke, millet floor and a few sweet potatoes through a couple who would occasionally travel to their village from the city to check on their farm. Every weekend, Maanz's father would be on the lookout for them, and if they came to the village, they would carry some food stuff for Maanzi. Maanzi made a friend in this couple for life.

Towards the end of the holiday, there was no supply of food from home. There were no phones, no communication. If the good Samaritan did not show up at school on the weekend, it automatically meant that he had not travelled to the village. Maanzi did not want to become a burden, on several occasions, he would walk to the household of this couple in the city and get some food and carry left overs to school.

For the last week of the holiday, there was no food, Maanzi survived on boiled water and tea leaves. Despite this, he and his handful of friends, who looked like ghosts in a human shells, continued to meet up in this one open classroom where they studied day and night. No one spoke, they each were like haunted men. One of these students, Maanzi later learned, had secured himself a great gig. He had been allowed by the school to always stay during the holidays and maintain the school compound in exchange for his fees. He obviously did not earn enough to pay his school fees, but one of the teachers had lobbied the school for him. Maanzi knew this because, he tried to ask for this job from the academic secretary.

As the week was ending, Maanzi was starving, he was dizzy and felt very week.

"I think I am going to die from hunger, I have to do something, I need to eat, at least a meal to keep me for the next two days until the school opens officially," Maanzi thought.

So Maanzi decided to visit a hotel which was near their school. There was one problem though, there were always guards at the gate and they would not allow him inside with no reason.

So he decided to enter through the sewerage pipes, good thing it was a dry season and the journey through was not that bad. Under the cover of darkness, he rushed out of the shadows and mingled with the 'rich people' of the city who had been attending a concert at this hotel by a local musician.

Maanzi immediately saw a family leaving a table, where they had been dinning. He rushed there and started to eat what was left over. He moved to another table and cleared it as well, putting his jackpot prize into a plastic bag and headed into the shadows. Once he emerged from the sewerage pipes, on the other side of the hotel, he found a place on the ground and ate all his food. It tasted like nothing he had ever eaten before. Maanzi does not remember what type of leftover food it was but saved his life.

He scraped the bones and ate anything else that he could chew and swallow. Afterwards, he headed back to school, to class. And the second day after this, was the school's official opening day. He was ready for the last term.

Chapter 16

WHILE MAANZI WAS AWAY AT THE 'PRESTIGIOUS' SECONDARY school, struggling but happy to be in school, Zuri was in Form 2 in the secondary school near her home in their village.

She had been warned by her friends at school about hanging out with the teacher, but somehow, she thought they were being envious of her academic success and social position. For Zuri, it was the first time in her life someone cared for her and was interested in her life.

"You are very intelligent and beautiful, Zuri, and you have a bright future," James repeatedly told her. "I will help you with anything you want to succeed," he said.

Anything, Zuri thought to herself. *Someone sees my potential, and he is in a position to actually help.*

"I will also do anything you ask me to do if you would help me and guide me to become a teacher," Zuri promised James.

She wasn't sure when it all started, but she began to realize that she would tire more quickly. By the end of the day, even when she hadn't done particularly heavy work, she simply was tired. Initially, she blamed it on a cold that she had recently suffered. Maybe that was it. But somehow, even when that cleared up, she was still weary; getting up in the morning was getting harder and harder.

I must be coming down with malaria, she thought.

But she also had a growing appetite. She would wake up in the middle of the night and quietly go to the kitchen to eat leftovers from the evening meal. Soon she began hiding food in her room, after a close encounter with her mother in the kitchen.

What is happening to me? Zuri thought, feeling an uneasy wave as she tried on her school uniform one morning. It barely fitted her.

It was her friend Kamaranzi who pointed out, "Your chest is growing bigger and you are gaining a lot of weight. Are you pregnant?"

Shock! "What? No!" she protested as her mind went a million ways; she felt her heart sink and her feet give way. Her grandmother had a saying for when someone felt like this; she said, "You feel like your gut is flowing out of your body." Zuri was sweaty and dizzy and took a while to realize that Kamaranzi had moved on to the next topic and was saying that they needed to hurry to go to the next class.

It was a math class, that much she knew, but what was discussed in that class and the remainder of the day remained a blur. She was stunned into silence. *Dear God, what did I do to deserve this?* Oh, the fear and shame. She could see it now. She had heard about girls who were sent to school and got pregnant. She had hoped that she would not be one of them. A string of thoughts ran through her mind: *What names will people call me? How will they react to this? What will I do?* Zuri knew that if people were kind to her, they would say she was ungrateful.

"You saw what your parents went through and still did not commit to study hard. Instead, you run around with men." This could be the neighbour the next day.

But her parents—dear God, her parents—the things they would say to her, the ridicule they would have to endure from the people in the village; she couldn't think that far.

That evening after school, Zuri veered off the main path into the bushes and fell onto the ground.

"Dear God, what is going on, and what is going to happen to me?" she cried aloud. "How do I go home and face my parents? If Kamaranzi was able to tell that something was going on, my mother may already know, but why hasn't she said anything yet? Maybe this is not true, but I have missed two menstrual periods, something is wrong." Zuri continued to sob.

That night, her mother did not say anything to her, so she decided to keep quiet and stay in school as usual.

While in class the next day, Kamaranzi would be stealing a glance at her most of the time, and she felt uneasy.

Oh, dear God. What have I done? she thought, sinking into depression yet still too stunned to cry. Her hands were shaking as she pretended to follow what the teacher was saying. *Dear Lord, what have I done? How could I be so stupid!* she repeated to herself over and over again.

Her grandmother was a pessimist and had warned her, "Be careful of excessive joy, there usually is great sorrow right behind it." This was what she had told her the day Zuri had met James. He was helping her with school work and also helping with the school fees, and she did not have to be chased from school anymore for unpaid dues.

She went home in a daze and did her chores as always, but quietly. When her younger sister, Judith, asked if they could both play with her dolls, she snapped at her like she never had before. Judith ran away, heartbroken that her big sister had been so rude and unkind to her. When she felt tired, she pushed herself. She didn't want her parents suspecting anything. Not yet, at least until she had a plan.

That night, the haze began to clear, and she began to realize the gravity of her situation. She felt horrible. Indeed, there was no one to blame; she had been warned, and yet she had still gone ahead. Now her future was bleak. The school suspended any girls who were pregnant; therefore, there was no hope of staying in school, for a short time, anyway.

"You know that it's not worth spending money educating girls," her father had once said when her mother advocated for her fees to be paid in full.

"We could sell the small goat and pay Zuri's fees so that she can sit for her exams," her mother had suggested.

"Are you not aware of what happens to girls when stubborn and foolish parents like you spend their money on them? They always disappoint them. They get pregnant," Jackson snapped. It was a cultural phenomenon for people in Uganda to hold women to high standards when it came to pregnancy and childbirth. Pregnancy was thought of as a woman's *thing*, even when it really took two people to make a pregnancy. The majority of Ugandan society even accepted this as a norm. If a woman got pregnant in school, she was chased out. The boy or her partner could continue to study without any remorse or sense of responsibility.

"How can this continue? Why are women blamed for their pregnancy and not men?" This was one of Maanzi's frustrations, and he hoped to work to change this perception and practice when he advocated for sexual and reproductive health rights.

"Please give her a chance, please. Until now, she has continued to do well and has not disappointed us. Please," Kesiime pleaded with Jackson, her husband.

While Zuri was washing the dishes after dinner, she asked her father about the last school fees installment.

"Dad," she said, "they have chased me from school for the last bit of money."

Her father had looked at his daughter, stood up, and walked out to find his wife on the veranda.

"We do not have any more money for Zuri," he said. "She is old enough for marriage, and at least she has studied more than the average girls in the village. I do not want to get disappointed. We know what becomes of such girls."

Jackson would have stopped the fees at that time, had it not been Zuri's mother's pleading.

"I will go and ask Mr. Enock to come and take that small goat for slaughter tomorrow," he said. "Your daughter had better do what she has promised to do, study, and not just go there to get pregnant. And if she gets pregnant, it will totally be your fault."

Zuri's father, with sadness in his voice, went off to look for Enock, the butcher man.

"Thank you, Mother," Zuri said when she emerged from the kitchen.

"Do not thank me, just go to school and work hard, and do not bring tears to my eyes one day," her mother continued. "I hope that I will not regret this decision."

The day had come; this conversation from the distant past came flooding into Zuri's mind, painful and piercing so sharply to her heart. "I am so sorry, Mother," she said quietly. "I should not have tried to even dream that things would be different."

If only the ground would swallow her right now. It would be easier if she could wake up dead. Dear God, what had she done? She wept over and over again.

She slept fitfully that night, and it was as the sun was rising that she devised a plan. She would go to the teacher and let him know what had happened. He had always been kind and understanding. He wasn't married, so maybe she could move to his home and have the child, and then he could support her studies. Yes, that is what she would do, she thought. But fear still ran deep. She knew what happened to girls who got pregnant out of wedlock. On a rare occasion, the father of the baby would agree to marry her. But usually, this happened for the girls who were already planning to marry the man, and if she got pregnant, the wedding was brought forward. More often than not, however, the father of the child denied any association with the woman. Her family was shamed, and she was married off to a man in a distant village. How she prayed that her situation would be different.

She was early for school that day and made a bee-line for the staff room. She had not seen their history teacher in a week, but that was common, as he did not tell her when he came and went. She met the math teacher and asked where the history teacher was.

"I thought he left already," he said.

"What do you mean?" Zuri asked.

"He was transferred in the middle of the term to a school in Kabale since the headteacher in that school recently passed away," he replied.

This could not be happening. What was he saying? Problems did not come alone... they came in threes, Zuri thought.

"Did he take all his things?" she asked, unwilling to give up any hope that she would not see him again.

"He left some things, but we don't know when he will be back for them. Probably during the holidays. Did you need me to help you with anything?" he asked.

"No thanks," she said as she walked away.

Where was she to go? He had been transferred to a place she only heard of but had never gone to. There was no money to get there, and how could she travel by herself? She had never left home. How would she tell her parents that she was going after a man? No, this was the end of her dreams. Since it was still early, and the majority of the students were yet to come, she walked to the edge of the school compound, hid next to a tree, and cried her eyes out. She prayed for a miracle that would somehow right the wrongs, that by some miracle she would be saved from a life she dreaded, the life that she had seen her mother endure. She prayed for anything and everything that came to mind.

It took her three weeks to work up the courage to break the news to her mother.

It's the only way. I have to tell her, Zuri told herself. *She will help me to convince my father; she always does.*

So one morning, after her brothers had rushed off to school, she told her mother, "I don't feel like going to school today."

"Are you ill?" her mother asked with a look of concern.

She looked down at her feet, wishing over and over again that the ground would swallow her. "No, I'm pregnant," she replied quietly.

"What?" her mother replied in disbelief.

"No, no, no no," her mother vigorously shaking her head as if to awake from a very bad dream.

"Please don't ever use that P word in here."

"Please tell me it is not true," her mother was covering her face by this time, tears rolling like a stream.

"My daughter, what have you done? "

"Eeeh, my dear Lord, what shall I do, what shall I say?" Zuri's mother was pacing back and forth, talking to herself and could not hold her overwhelming grief from her daughter.

She then suddenly wiped her face, stopped talking and looked straight into her daughter's eyes.

"I was such a fool. Your father should have married you off." She burst out.

She was angry. That much Zuri knew and expected, but the words hurt just the same.

"You know?" Zuri asked, shocked. Her mom looked at her with eyes full of sorrow, with a face of resignation.

"You have been gaining weight and your neck veins have been beating so fast," her mother replied. "I defended you. I have been fighting your father to allow you to stay in school."

"My child loves school and would never do that," her mother had once told a neighbour's wife, who asked her why she insisted that her daughter stays in school while there was plenty of woman's work at home she could help with.

"How could you do this to me?" she asked again, teary-eyed and not giving her time to respond. "Don't you know how we suffered to raise the money for school fees? Do you have any idea what your father is going to do with you? To both of us, when he hears about it?" On and on she went.

But it was the last thing she said that would finally break Zuri's façade. She had promised herself that she would not cry...

"You were supposed to do better than me. Education was supposed to take you places.

"My girl, will at least get an education, get a glimpse of what I was never allowed to have, she will change her life, she will live better than I did," her mother said.

Now I see that I was just such a fool, to have ever put my hope in you against your father's judgement. How I fought him day and night, how I felt proud of you when the village women complained about my heavy load at home and you going to school. It is my fault." Zuri's mother sat down on the ground, in front of their small house and held her face in her hands and cried for a while. Two of her young children were pulling at her from behind, distraught to see their mother crying, "Mommy, Mommy, stop crying," they cried.

Now you will end up like me if you're lucky. Most likely worse. Who is going to want to marry you after they hear about this?" Zuri's mother cried.

"Don't you think I get it? Don't worry, it will be my life, not yours," Zuri replied impudently.

"You think I am happy when you are not? Do you think that just because I didn't go to school, I have no feelings? I felt pain all those days when I needed your help, and I would watch you watch your brothers with longing since you wanted to be in school. Never think for one second that your life is yours alone. I do care about you, and I hurt when you hurt. Even now, I wish I could take your place so that you would not suffer what I am sure you are going to suffer. Life of a woman, in this part of the world with no education, is a life of misery, a life of no options, a life that I hoped my children would never have to face." She was now stern-faced.

She had felt alone and cried a million times over the life that was soon to be her reality but to have her mother say these words… it meant the world to her.

"Come over here, you fool," her mother stood up and stretched her arms wide open.

She hugged her, and they wept together. She wasn't one to display emotions but realized that her child needed it.

"What did we do to deserve this?" Zuri's mother asked as she wept.

The two women settled for what was inevitable to happen that evening, Jackson will hear about this, and god save the cat and the dog, or even the mouse in the house that night!

As had been predicted, Jackson was livid when his wife quietly told him what had transpired. It was evening, and everyone had come home from school. He had brought in the few remaining cattle from grazing, and after he had had a cup of black tea with no sugar while listening to the radio in the compound, Zuri's mother had asked that they go to the house, as she had something to tell him. She knew she had to tell him in private because if he was near Zuri the first time he heard the news, he would hit her. Pregnant or not, he would hit her, and who knows how this would turn out for her and the child.

"I told you it was a bad idea to invest money in educating a girl," he said.

"You are to blame for your daughter's behaviour and disgrace," he continued.

"You defended her ridiculous idea to stay in school, and now you see what has happened? Do you know how many cows I could have bought instead?"

Her mother kept quiet. She had learned over the years that to respond when he was in this state would be to invite more trouble than it was worth.

"Now see what a disgrace she has become. Who do you think is going to marry your daughter? Who?"

Funny how she had asked her daughter the same things. He yelled a bit more as he paced around the small room. She looked through the wooden window that was only slightly open and saw that the other children were listening attentively. Zuri was by herself, a little separate from the rest.

"No wonder she was so determined to go to school every day. She was all along looking for men," he continued.

His frustration was difficult to explain. She had thought part of him would be relieved now that he didn't have to pay school fees for her anymore. But his reaction, though expected, was a bit much. She could see that he was deeply bothered, and there was no sign of relief. His eyes carried much pain.

Had he also secretly hoped that his daughter would have a better life?

Was he now disappointed? Or was he simply mad that since she had become pregnant, her dowry would be less?

"Who is the father anyway?" Zuri's father asked.

Zuri's mother had not asked, as she had been overwhelmed and so afraid thinking of the father's reaction that somehow, she had forgotten to get this little bit of information.

"Well?" he asked, waiting for her to answer.

"I didn't ask," she replied.

"You didn't ..." He stared at her in disbelief. "You and your child... call your daughter and let her explain."

She didn't need to call, as Zuri had been outside, listening to everything that was transpiring in the house (together with all the passersby).

"It was one of the teachers at school," Zuri said quietly.

"He has been transferred to another school very far away." She continued.

"Of course, he has," her father replied. "How convenient."

But the mother was silent for a minute, with a puzzled expression on her face, as if trying to figure out something in her mind yet not quite believing the conclusions she came to.

"So the scholarship you said you had got was not really from school but this man. Right?" her mother finally said.

Zuri stared at her father, afraid and wishing that she could lie to them but not quite able to bring herself to that point.

"Yes, Mother," she replied.

"I was desperate, I wanted to continue schooling, and you, you" her lips quivering "you were trying so much but were not able to get the money."

"It was stupid of me, but that promised to further my education," she regretted.

She could see with understanding what they were thinking. There were also names for girls that got these kinds of favours from men. Horrible names... but she had told herself she wasn't one of them. This was different.

"I was desperate," she dared to explain, not knowing that she was digging her own grave even further and nailing her coffin. "He promised me that he was just helping me because I had a future, and I trusted him."

"Of all the ..." Jackson caught himself before he could say any other thing.

"Go. Just go." Zuri's father seemed tired, resigned, as if he had aged a decade in the last thirty minutes. "I guess you are old enough now to have your own children and family," he concluded, as though he needed to hurt her one last time for all the hurt she had caused him.

She went away and wept—wept as she had never wept before, as though all the nights she'd cried herself to sleep because of this had simply been a rehearsal for this one final moment. She had thought that there was only so far down that one could fall. But it was as though each day showed her that there were deeper depths and greater hurts that her heart would endure. What hurt her most, was the pain and hurt she had seen on her parents' faces that night.

Now that she had told her parents, even though they were mad at her, she was relieved. But everywhere she went, whether to fetch water or to the trading centers, there were stares and whispers. She once had hoped to be an example of what happens when you educate a girl. Now she was the humiliation and the reasons why 'intelligent' parents from this part of the world should not take their girls to school. It was a waste of money, especially for one who seemingly had a bright future.

She returned to school after the weekend, but this was not to last forever. One day, she was called to the headmaster's office. She knew what this was about. Everyone in the school knew. Everyone was waiting for this day; it's what happens. A girl gets pregnant, she gets dismissed from school, disowned by her parents. The boy continues to study, and graduates, or even if he does not graduate, life moves on, he gets another girl and gets married. No one ever asks him, "how about that girl whose life you ruined".

"This school does not tolerate indiscipline of this kind. We train pupils, not women," the headteacher said as he handed her a letter of dismissal. "Here, take this to your parents. You are not accepted in school anymore."

As she stood up to leave his office, the headteacher called out to her, "Zuri, I surely hoped you would do better than this; you had a great future ahead of you. That's all. There is nothing I can now do for you."

The headteacher bent forward and put his hands across his head. He was one of the few who believed in equal opportunities in school for boys and girls.

He lamented why the school did not have a way of supporting those such as Zuri who was struggling so much financially and showing promise. *We have to do better than this. What would I do if this were my little girl?* he thought to himself.

The next day, he announced at the school assembly, "Zuri was expelled from school yesterday because she is pregnant. That should act as a warning to all of you girls who, instead of concentrating on your studies, are here to run after men and boys. This school will not tolerate this behaviour."

Her school friends no longer wanted to be associated with her and would ignore her if they met along the way or at the well. Her younger brother, Martin, who had previously loved to play with her, now no longer wanted anything to do with her.

"Your sister is a disgrace to all of us," some boy had told her young brother, and he felt offended but also embarrassed.

Martin immediately put down his pot of water, moved very fast and furiously pushed the pot of water off this boy's head. It came crashing down in pieces and water splashing everywhere. The boy burst out in a loud cry and ran home so fast to report this incident to his parents.

Martin headed home, with rage that someone should say that about his sister. He did not say anything to his parents.

"Do you know what your son did today?" the boy's mother came running and in a foul mood with her son following behind.

She was carrying with her some pieces of the broken water pot. "See what your son did to my pot, he broke it on top of my son's head. Can you explain this to me?" She demanded of Zuri and Martin's mother Kesiime.

"Martin, Martin, come here right now," his mother was calling. Martin came out of the kitchen.

"Explain to me what happened about this pot. Are you running mad? Why did you break the pot on this boy's head?" she demanded.

Martin, looking on the ground and not maintaining eye contact, responded, "he was calling Zuri names and making fun of her".

The boy's mother felt ashamed and turned to her son, "What did you say about his sister? Go home, I will come following you and you will tell me exactly what you said."

She then turned to Zuri's mother and apologized, "I am sorry, Kesiime. These boys can get out of hand sometimes; I will deal with him. I know things are not ideal at this time with you." She turned and headed back to her home.

Kesiime turned to her son Martin, "I know you were trying to defend your sister, but don't go around the village breaking people's water pots on their heads. Leave this issue to me and your father. Now go and do your homework, then come out and help with the chores."

"Hey, do you need help with your homework?" Zuri would ask.

"No, thank you," he replied. Martin felt betrayed by his sister because she had become a joke at school.

"Has your sister given birth yet? Are you an uncle?" pupils would tease him.

Zuri felt alone, isolated, betrayed, and disoriented. She contemplated ending it all many times but could not bring herself to do it; besides, that would mean going to the old traditional birth attendants who would give you herbs, and she did not want that. Besides, everyone already knew. Her life, her dreams, her future had come to an untimely end, an end that she knew was final. She was afraid of what would happen to her and the unborn baby.

Zuri never received prenatal care, as was common for girls in her situation. While the majority of married pregnant women in the community would at least attend one session of prenatal care at the local clinic, she did not attend any. Not even once. The reasons were the same. There was no money to attend prenatal care. Even though this was considered free at the health center, one needed money for transport costs and the prescriptions she would receive once she attended. Since her mother had never attended any prenatal care and had managed to deliver five healthy babies, she did not see the reasons why this was needed.

One day, Zuri said, "Mother, I would like to go for prenatal care at the local clinic tomorrow for a checkup."

"Local clinic? Why? You should start eating the brown soil behind the kitchen, rub the cow butter on your belly and pelvic bones, and do not eat eggs or drink milk; these will make your baby too big for you. That's all you need. I need help here, so do not be going away and leaving me with all the work."

Maanzi returned home for the holiday at the end of his high school. After dropping his bags and saying a few pleasantries to his parents, he headed to Zuri's household. There was so much he had to tell her about his new school and how the rich children conducted themselves. Oh, the stories he had to tell and the stories that he could never tell. He hadn't heard the news. No one bothered to tell him because they knew that he would learn soon enough. It was a very painful topic for anyone to bring up voluntarily.

To say that he was shocked when he saw his friend laying pregnant, on a mat, on the floor in their house would be an understatement. Zuri looked pale, had grossly swollen feet, and was obviously pregnant. She seemed to be in pain and had a horrible cough that did not allow her to rest, as every few minutes, she would have a coughing spell and hold onto her tummy. The veins of her neck grew prominent and her eyes would turn red from the cough. She was ill, obviously ill, and sad. So very sad.

She managed to fake a smile for him when she saw him.

"Hi," she said, as she slowly supported herself to get up.

Maanzi had simply been frozen for a moment, trying to comprehend what had happened and trying to take it all in, as a deep sadness began to take root in his heart.

"Hi," he replied, not knowing what else to say.

"Wha... whaaa—" He had to clear his throat before the words could come out more clearly. "What happened?" he asked.

With no words, her tears began to fall freely as his own eyes barely restrained tears. They didn't have to talk about it, as they both knew exactly what would become of Zuri's future and education.

They both moved to the verandah and leaned against the mud walls of the kitchen, trying to get into the comfort of the shade. As they both gazed into the nothingness of the cloud-covered sky, the clouds were covering and revealing the setting sun. Maanzi dared say nothing at all to her, so there was waiting and silence. Zuri broke the silence and began to speak without giving her dear friend eye contact.

"He promised me that he would pay my school fees until I finished college," Zuri started. "It was toward the end of the term; my father had not even paid a single coin. So, I was chased from school and spent a few days home. I walked over to his house, and he was there marking student's work. He stood up, welcomed me, and asked where I had been."

"It is towards the end of the school term, and I have not seen you in class, is everything okay?" The teacher had asked. And he looked deeply concerned.

Maanzi said, "And what happened?"

"He said that he was going to pay for all the school fees that term."

"What? Really?"

Zuri, with tears running down, remembered hugging him and saying very many thank-yous.

"There is, however, one thing that you have to do for me first," James had said.

"Anything, anything," Zuri narrated. "I thought he was going to ask me to fetch water or help cook his meals or something else. No, he was every inappropriate with me. He told me that if I refused, there would be no more school fees, no more plans of going to teacher's college.

"'You will not get pregnant, I will make sure of it,' he had promised."

Zuri now sobbing uncontrollably.

"He promised, Maanzi. He promised he would not get me pregnant. He ruined my future, my life. Many days, I want to end it all." Zuri turned, looked at his cousin and again looked away immediately, drying her tears.

Maanzi was quiet, his throat choking with rage and anger at the teacher.

She had no fighting chance. She was going to have to give birth with the help of the traditional birth attendant.

If she was lucky, she would be married soon, definitely not for love, oh no... but to the first man who asked. Usually, a drunk, whom the "good girls" in the village had rejected or a very poor man who could not afford the dowry that the other girls' parents had demanded. She would work on the farm and give birth to more children, half a dozen or more, probably more because contraception was not readily available, but even if it were, there were social and cultural barriers to contraceptive use. She would give birth to many children. Because with no education, she would have no rights to her body and reproductive decisions.

They continued to speak for a while. Zuri filled him in on the details about the baby's father.

"You know, James was a dreamer. He told me about schools in the city, the life there, and life in college. He came back last month to collect his belongings from his house. My brother Martin told me that he had said his official good-byes at the school assembly that morning. So, I rushed to his house that evening to see him ..."

Maanzi interrupted, "And did you see him and tell him about the pregnancy?"

"Yes, I saw him. You won't believe what he told me." In a male voice, Zuri said, "I don't think that is my responsibility. It cannot be my child, I was careful. Are you sure it is not another man's child?"

"Another man's child indeed," Zuri said in her normal voice, wiping away her tears again.

"I now have a new life in a new place," she continued in the male voice, "and I do not want to complicate it with having to support you. I am also planning to get married to one of the teachers in my new school."

Maanzi reached out and held Zuri's hand, and they sat silently for a long time.

"And the headteacher did nothing to this teacher?" Maanzi finally asked. "This kind of injustice must be addressed. People like James should be held responsible. It is just not fair."

After a while, it was time for Maanzi to return to his parents' house.

"I am happy you are here," Zuri said, hugging Maanzi.

They couldn't go anywhere, as Zuri was to be hidden from the public eye; Maanzi wondered whether the small, cramped room with dust from the dirt floors was instead making her more ill and depressed.

By the time he left, Maanzi was broken-hearted, frustrated, angry, hopeless, and helpless. But who was he angry at? He was angry at the social and cultural inequalities that had held his people backward, especially the women. He was angry that the man who had made his cousin pregnant was not taking any responsibility and perhaps had gone on with his life without a care in the world. He was angry that this selfish man had taken advantage of Zuri's poverty and lack of school fees and then destroyed her future.

He felt a rush of emotions come back to him as he remembered the bicycle mechanic who took advantage of his helplessness and refused to pay for his pancakes. He had flashbacks of everyone there, laughing and cheering on the mechanic, with no care or regard for the young boy who was trying everything possible to raise money for his school fees.

It is a world where the powerful feed on the poor and weak without a care, Maanzi thought, *a world that Zuri and I thought we would change.* But what hurt him the most was that their world was unforgiving. One mistake, and your life was as good as done. There seemed no way to recover from it. If he failed his exams, he would be right where he started, maybe even worse off. Because she got involved with a man, granted a big mistake and granted she had been warned but was that justification enough for her dreams to end at such a young age? He found himself tearing up most of the time; his heart was heavy, and he could swear he was having severe chest pain. He almost needed pain killers for it.

He was unsettled that, while he was able to continue to struggle on in school and with each term he was getting closer to his goal, Zuri would not; at that moment, he wished his cousin was a boy.

"You should go back to school after your baby is born," Maanzi said as they spoke one afternoon. He had convinced her to carry her mat outside into the grass so that she could get some sunshine. But she only agreed because her parents had gone to a funeral a way off, and it was unlikely that they would be home soon. Otherwise, there would be hell to pay. He was unwilling to give up all hope that her dreams were gone. She looked at him sadly, wondering why he seemed to need to inflict this pain, as he knew as much as she did the reasons why this was not possible. She was silent as she stared at him.

"It's just not fair. If I complete my school, get a job, maybe one day I could take care of you," he said. "Maybe support you to go back to school. I am thinking of studying to become a doctor."

"Don't laugh, I know it is a big dream, but I will try my best," Maanzi said.

"A doctor?" Zuri asked, ignoring everything else that had been said. Life was too uncertain, and hope was painful. "A doctor with jiggers in his feet," she said, and they both laughed.

"What happened to the lawyer thing?" Zuri asked, a bit confused. Maanzi ignored the question.

It was good, as there had not been much to laugh about.

"Let me check to make sure that your feet have no jiggers. We do not want you to go off to university with jiggers," Zuri joked. "So, do you think you will pass your exam?" Zuri asked with concern in her voice and eyes.

"Life has been very difficult in high school for me. There are stories that I could tell you and you will never believe, and there are stories I could never tell. I read every single day and gave it my best, there is nothing else I could have done," Maanzi said.

"I don't know what I will do if I fail this exam. My parents have given all, sold all the goats, cows and family land. I will just wait." Maanzi concluded, "For now, I will keep working and raising some money, who knows what may happen. If I pass, I will need transportation. I am really hoping to get a government scholarship, then my parents do not have to worry about me anymore.

"You will be okay. Life cannot be cruel to both of us at the same time," Zuri replied.

"Yeah," Maanzi agreed.

Why did we think that we could dream? Why did we ever imagine that we could escape this village that seems to be a prison with no fences? Why did we think that our lives could be any different? Maanzi was thinking to himself. The future without him passing his exam was an abyss.

Maanzi was big support that holiday and her days were brightened as she thought about his daily visits. While the initial visits were heavy as he came to terms with her situation, he seemed to have taken it upon himself to make her smile. So, he told her stories about his new school and about the things he encountered.

He filled her in on what was happening in and around the village, but best of all, he treated her just the same, and she was grateful for that. She could tell from the polite talk of some of the relatives how many thought that she had been marred by what she had done. So, whenever anyone spoke to her as they had previously, she was grateful.

The situation, however, confirmed to Maanzi that he was indeed pursuing the right career. He would use his career to care and advocate for vulnerable people who were in difficult positions and perhaps make a difference. If it was not too late, he would maybe pay school fees for her, to further her education as well.

There was lots of work to be done to make the situation of rural women better. They were born in difficult circumstances, but no one seemed to care or wanted to help them. He knew he was making an unfair judgment of the country's leader, who had been applauded for doing a lot to improve the circumstances and education for girls in the country, but somehow that wasn't enough. At the time, education, eradication of poverty, maternal and child health issues had been on top of the political agenda.

It had been announced that girls were to be given an extra 1.5 points on top of what they scored at the university entrance exams so that more girls would be eligible to enter university. But it was rare that you failed to get into university because you lacked just 1.5 points. The policy would mainly serve to favour a department to pick a girl rather than a boy if the two had scored the same. There was a woman vice president for the first time in the country, and another first was that there were new women representatives who served in the parliament from every district. They were supposed to represent women's rights. Maanzi argued that this only served to bring politics closer to the people but did not lead to real change. The few organizations that were actually bringing change did not favour the girls in rural areas. Some provided scholarships exclusive to girls, but these were based upon their scores at the national exams.

But how was someone in the rural areas supposed to compete favourably, especially if their schools did not have libraries, and their teachers did not speak standard English, the language in which these exams were written?

How were girls like Zuri supposed to benefit from the extra 1.5 points the government was giving at the end of high school when the majority were unable to complete primary education due to lack of financial support?

There were small issues that could be quickly resolved, but somehow even the women representatives in parliament never did address them. Why were pregnant girls expelled from school simply for being pregnant, yet nothing happened to the boys and men responsible? Was it even necessary for pregnant girls to be expelled? Why weren't girls and boys in the same family both pro-vided with equal opportunities for education?

Most women in his village could be described as, being born to only grow up, get married, and have children; this was prestigious for their husbands. They looked after the children and worked long hours in the gardens with little to no appreciation. Some were mistreated by their husbands, but they were not allowed to talk about it. Women continued to die in pregnancy and childbirth; it was considered a curse by the gods for their misconduct, such as having an extramarital affair. Men, on the other hand, if they struggled hard, could obtain a slightly higher level of education, and then their parents were culturally obliged to give them a piece of the family land, build a house for them, and pay a dowry for their wife. Then the wife would take care of the children they bore, while men if they had a few heads of cattle, would tend to the cows and once in a while help in the gardens.

During this long holiday after high school, Maanzi continued to work hard as he awaited his results, trying to save as much money as he could for university. He had been taught to be polite to people. He would go from shop to shop, selling pancakes with another cousin, who was also carrying a bag of wild passion fruits. The money they earned was meant to supplement their school fees. Maanzi would also collect his money from his debtors. A good day of sales would make him 200 Uganda shillings (equivalent to almost ten cents). He would have had to make 200 pieces of pancakes. After high school, the whole trade was handed over to him, he knew how to make the pancakes and his parents simply helped. It had become his sole responsibility and he took it seriously.

Many of the shopkeepers would ask for pancakes and would say, "I will pay you later," but at the end of the day, they would more often than not tell him, "I have not sold anything in my shop today, come back tomorrow." But at least they were not as rude as the mechanic. These games taught him patience, persistence, and perseverance; he learned that if you do not get something the first time, you simply have to keep working at it, until it happens, or it becomes apparent that the situation is futile.

Maanzi was about to have another encounter that he would never forget. An encounter that his father had helped him to put in perspective as he goes through life.

One particularly hot afternoon, two middle-aged gentlemen cycled past Maanzi and his cousin Joseph as they walked the muddy path to the trading center. The two cousins were already loaded with their merchandise and looked longingly as the men rode by since neither of them was carrying anything on their bicycles. Since it was a small village, and everyone knew everyone, it was common practice that someone would give you a ride, especially if they were not carrying anything on their bicycle. The men did not even care to greet them, but the two cousins shouted their hellos as they had been taught.

When the two men reached a steep slope, Maanzi and Joseph looked at each other and gently ran after the men on their bicycles, taking care not to spill the goods in the baskets on their heads. As the men were disembarking from their bicycles, they approached them with so much enthusiasm.

"Good evening, Sirs," said the boys in unison. "Can we help you push your bicycles uphill?"

"Good evening, boys. Sure, you can push the bicycles. But do not ride them."

The men gave them bicycles and continued to be engaged in their conversation. The cousins rested their goods on the bicycle carriers as they pushed the bicycles fast up the hill and waited for the owners, half hoping that the men would return the favour and carry them to the shops since they were all headed that way. At the top of the hill, the gentlemen were still immersed in their conversation. The first man got on his bicycle and invited Joseph to jump on for a ride.

"Hey, jump on, let me give you a ride to the shops," he said.

Maanzi assumed the gentleman had spoken for his friend. So, he steadied his pancakes on his head, and with his free hand, held and jumped onto the second man's bicycle, but he suddenly choked the brakes and asked, "Who told you to jump on the bicycle?"

"Uh, ah uh, sorry sir," he immediately replied.

But he remained sitting on the bicycle, hoping he would change his mind.

"I thought that since your friend carried my cousin, and after pushing your bicycle up the hill, you would give me a ride to the shops," Maanzi replied, feeling very humiliated.

"Get down from my bicycle," the man demanded.

"Your father does not own a bicycle," the gentleman continued.

"Perhaps you should walk until he can afford his own bicycle."

Then he added sarcastically, "If only he was not selling off his land and wasting his money on those expensive schools."

Maanzi quickly jumped down, and the gentleman rode off without looking back, only mumbling more words to himself that Maanzi did not care to hear.

This incident was a bitter reminder of the struggles that his parents were facing to keep him in school. His father had elucidated to such encounters every day as he worked in people's farms, or as he sold pancakes or bananas, or rock salt in the marketplace to raise money for fees. He was reminded yet again of the sacrifices they had made and the struggles that people like himself and Zuri had to overcome to forge a better future for themselves and their families.

Maanzi continued to walk, head down, hoping that this would end soon. After a while, Joseph looked back, and when he could not see him with the other gentleman, he got off the first man's bicycle and waited for him.

"What happened?" Joseph asked.

"He told me to get off his bicycle," Maanzi replied. He said that I should wait until my father can afford a bicycle."

"Mean man; we shall never help him push his bicycle again," said Joseph.

"We will walk, as usual. We always do, don't we?"

"We will buy our own bicycles when we grow up, and buy more for our parents," Maanzi replied with a half-smile.

"Who needs to sit on these old looking rusty bicycles anyway," joked Joseph.

Maanzi knew that the gentleman had spoken the reality, the truth, what was prevailing at the time. But he was determined to work and defy the odds, change that reality, and change the perception of the people about educating their children. This fueled his determination and resolve.

But this event stirred a whirlwind of emotions inside Maanzi; he knew that he had worked so hard at school, but he feared that if he did not make it into the university, this was to be his life, a life of being pulled off someone's bicycle, a life of being ridiculed because his father was sacrificing to put him through school and wanted a better life for him. He had to make it. Hmm, now, he would have to buy his father a bicycle, to shame the gentleman who disgraced his father for not being able to afford one. All he wanted was to work hard and change the reality that he had been born into.

That day, as they walked to and from the local shops, Maanzi was awfully quiet, and this worried Joseph, who asked him, "Why is your face downcast? Are you still thinking about that mad man?"

"No, I am worried about my high school results," he said. "I do not know what I will do if I fail my exams. My father has no more land to sell, both my parents have worked so hard, and I will never have another chance of attending high school. I have to pass."

"Why worry about it now?" his cousin answered. "Don't worry while you wait for the results. I am not sure how I will do myself in my end of secondary school." Joseph had also finished secondary school (Form 4), and he had also struggled with school fees and sold pancakes. "We just have to keep working hard and get ourselves through school."

"But just imagine you pass your exams and go to university. And soon you will become a doctor. Imagine how our lives could change. You will not only be able to afford a bicycle but a car, think about that, a car for Dr. Maanzi," Joseph was saying, trying hard to lighten his cousin's downcast soul.

Chapter 17

AS ZURI'S PREGNANCY CONTINUED, SHE GOT BIGGER. SHE WAS getting more tired easily and extremely weak. A traditional birth attendant had visited her occasionally to see how she was doing. This traditional birth attendant, who had named her 'Zuri', had helped her mother give birth to her, so she was going to help her and do the best she could to keep her and her baby safe. There were no plans of getting her into hospital for the birth, though she was just a teenager, with a risky pregnancy. There would be no money for things like this.

Maanzi was anxiously waiting for the results of the national exams that would determine whether or not he would go to university. These typically took about four months. He had taken to selling pancakes again during these long holidays as a way to save money for himself but also so that he would be able to support his parents as they raised money for his other siblings. One day, while Maanzi was at the local trading center going about his business, Josam, one of the wealthier people in the trading center, was seated outside his small shop, reading the local newspaper. Josam was considered well off by the village standards; he had at least seven bicycles because he also had more than four wives and dozens of cattle. He also had the very first brick and tin roof house in the trading center. He was a good customer and always bought pancakes for his many little children. Maanzi had established a good rapport with him.

"Sir, would you like some pancakes for the children today?" Maanzi would usually ask.

The newspaper had a story about some of the university entry candidates rejoicing with their parents after learning they passed their exams. He leaned over and started to read with the gentleman, his pancakes soon forgotten and his heart racing in anticipation. Had he done well? Over the last few months, he had agonized over the things he had forgotten while taking his exams; this had cost him a few sleepless nights. But this was it, finally. He would know for sure.

"Oh, that's right," the gentleman said, watching him with interest. "You sat your exams as well."

"Yes," Maanzi replied. He didn't have much to say as he scanned through the paper. The candidates who performed the best were from schools in the city. That was to be expected. While none of the students in his school were mentioned in the newspaper, there was a comment that they had performed well overall. Well, that was good news at least. There were no cell phones, so one could not telephone the school and find out their results.

He went home early that day, too excited to continue selling any more pancakes. These will have to wait, he thought to himself.

As he rushed home, he quickly thought over what he needed to do. The school would only release the results in person, but fortunately, he had saved enough money for transportation into the city to check for his results. He would get up early the next morning and trek to where he could catch a bus and head out there, or maybe he could ask Joseph to drop him on his father's bicycle. He was so excited and lost in thought, and it was a while before he realized he was home. His mother could tell something was up the moment she saw him.

"The results are out," he told her, a little excited and yet afraid to hope lest he was disappointed.

She swallowed hard. She was as scared as he was. Both parents had invested so much, and this was the moment of truth. Maanzi and his parents were all scared of what the results meant for the future of all of them. Would all their sacrifices pay off?

Francis, usually a man of few words, had even less to say that night as he headed to bed after hearing the news. Grace asked Maanzi if he had enough money for transportation costs and whether he had a place to stay overnight in case the bus was late. He said he had it all planned.

"We will pray for your journey," Grace said as they both headed to what they were sure would be a sleepless night.

That night, the house was very quiet, too quiet that one would think the family had received some kind of very bad news.

At dawn, Maanzi started his journey to the city. Soon after he got to the bus stop, a Matatu (minivan) arrived with twenty people in it, instead of the normal number of twelve. These were usually the best because since there were so many people on board, there would be fewer stops, and he had a greater chance of making it to the city and back that day. "Come and sit on my lap," one of the passengers said and motioned to Maanzi. So, he got on it, and off he went. He squeezed in right by the door, only part of his body on the kind passenger's lap. This was great, as he would have access to the windows, but that also meant he would be covered with dirt by the time he got to town, given that the road was so dusty. The lady next to him carried a live chicken. She had come from the city to visit her relatives in the village, and they rewarded her with a chicken, which would have been very expensive to buy in the town.

The minivan dropped him on the stage and he walked to the high school. It was in the midmorning and the school was quiet since the students were in their classrooms. His heart picked up a pace as he approached the administration block. Other students were standing outside, some were obviously happy and in jubilant moods, while others looked as apprehensive as Maanzi himself. He said hello and sat on the bench until it was his turn to go into the Director of Studies' office.

"Hello Maanzi, congratulations, you did very well, and in fact, you surprised most of us," the director said.

"Sit, sit, sit down," he motioned for him to have a sit. He then looked through a pile of result slips and pulled out his.

"There, you go. In fact, you did the best in your class of Biology, Physics, Maths, Chemistry." He looked pleased.

Maanzi was not in this place at this moment. He was far, far away, thinking of all the sacrifices, he could not laugh, he could not cry, he could not describe his deep emotion at this point. He was not aware of what the director of studies was saying to him from that moment on and for a few seconds; he took a journey back into time.

"What course did you apply for in university?" The director was asking him.

"Whaaat?" Maanzi seemed startled from his thoughts.

"Medicine, I applied for medicine."

"Well, there is no reason you should not get to do Medicine now. Best of luck. We are so proud of you as a school."

Maanzi reached for his result slip and headed out of the office, still in a haze of euphoria, he could not believe it. As he left the school compound, tears started rolling down his eyes. He whispered, "Dad, Mom, we made it. We passed our exams."

Even if I do not get enough points to do medicine on a government scholarship, I will be able to attend university and do another course on a government scholarship, he reassured himself as he headed to the taxi park to get a taxi back home.

When he arrived home that evening, his parents were both at home; his father had not gone to work that day, they were all awaiting the news.

"Mom, Dad, we passed," and Maanzi broke down crying so loudly that his mom Grace joined him.

Francis, his father, excused himself and took a walk to hide his emotions.

And just like that, the long journey had paid off. University education, on a government scholarship, was assured. What now remained was if he would make the cut-off points needed to do medicine. He had come so far, that even doing any course at the university, without his parents having to worry about affording it, was all he ever wanted, doing medicine would be his dream come true. *And who said that we cannot dream?* he thought.

Zuri was very excited and they both shed tears as he shared the results. His cousin Joseph was also over the moon.

"I told you that you would do well," I had no doubt. Now we wait for my results too. Joseph said. His excitement about his cousin's results was showing on his face, likely this gave him hope.

A few weeks passed, and the university selection process was complete. It was the moment of truth. The only two medical schools in the country at the time had produced their lists of the government-sponsored students who had met the cut points to be admitted. Lucky for him, Maanzi had put his choice to the Medical school near to his home because he thought to himself, *I could walk to university if I ever was not able to afford transport.* The privately sponsored students always placed their applications after the government-sponsored list was out. Maanzi did not bother himself with this list, because if he did not make the cut-off, he would have to forget medicine forever. There was no way of getting scholarships. He would then look at his second, third and fourth-course choices that he had applied for, just in case medicine did not work out.

The mood at home was jovial, many people in the village had come to know about his success. His mother and father talked about it, especially when people began to take them on for wasting money and embarrassing themselves looking for fees.

"Our sacrifices have paid off. Maanzi passed his high school exams. He is going to university," they would say.

"Oh, hmmm, okay. I did not know that" was usually one of the many answers coming from the ashamed person. That usually would be the end of the conversation about school. Many parents, though they did not outwardly talk about it, began to think and have a different view of giving their children a fighting chance at school, and were willing to do a bit more, or sacrifice a little to raise school fees.

When Maanzi learned that the results were out, and the lists were on the noticeboards displayed, he was gripped with a mixture of emotions, but he had waited his entire life, he had worked for this. He made the journey back to the city. Usually, the people in the taxi will talk about any and everything. Maanzi did not have any words, no conversations. He was squashed between people; the taxi was over packed, and he could barely feel his legs as the journey came to the close. His mind was already ahead of him, already at the university, scanning through the list of the names. With him thinking about the list, his mind was kept away from thinking about his pain and poor posturing.

He was dropped off a short distance from the university gates and had to wait a few minutes before he could recover the full use of his lower limbs, which had been squashed during the four-hour journey. After recovering, he headed to the university to look at the admission lists.

"Good afternoon, sir," he greeted the security man at the entrance. "Where is the admissions notice board?"

"Down to your right, then turn left, and it's the building with brown bricks in the center."

"Thank you, sir," replied Maanzi.

Excitement and uncertainty engulfed him as he approached the notice board; as he came close, he could see other applicants crowding around the board, looking for their names. He quickly picked up the pace, as did his heart; he broke through the bodies and gazed upon the printed lists. His eyes caught a familiar name, third place from the top on the list!

He had made it! It took a while to sink in as he read his name over and over and over and over again confirming that it was true. He made it. No, *they* made it ... his family and Uncle Jay and everyone else.

He stood at that notice board reading his name, hearing people rejoicing in the background. It was a moment he never wanted to forget. So much had led up to this moment, and here it was. The walking, living away from home, the selling pancakes, the games they played with Zuri trying to avoid school, selling property, his parents' sacrifices ... All that had led up to this final moment.

He recalled a particular conversation between his father and Uncle Jackson: "What makes you think your son can make it?" his uncle had asked.

"Do you think that he is any different from the rest of us?"

Finally, that would all be in the past. They had all accomplished their goal.

Before he turned to walk away, he looked at the board one last time, as if in the short while he had been there, his name could have been erased. He saw his name again. No, he wasn't dreaming; this was real, and they had collectively accomplished this.

After that, there was no stopping him. He could hardly wait to share the news with his parents, Zuri, and Uncle Jay. He was going to attend university on a government scholarship. He was going to do Medicine, yes Medicine and nothing was going to stop him from becoming a doctor now, except death itself.

He finally felt the rush of relief as he hurried to the station to take the next taxi home. He didn't even stop to eat anything, as he was way too excited to hold anything down; besides, his mind was going a mile a minute. He was going to be a doctor; that was a prestigious career. No one else in the village was a doctor. In fact, until this point in his life, he had not seen a doctor in the flesh. Because there was only one, maybe two for the whole district hospital, where he had been as a child, where he saw a child die waiting in the queue, where he saw a woman being taken out after having died in labour.

He vowed to himself as he waited for the bus that he would help his parents pay school fees for his siblings. He was also going to buy back the land that had been sold so that he would attend high school, and he was going to help Zuri go back to school.

As he got on the taxi, he realized this would be hard work, but he did not mind; working hard was already his second nature. A government scholarship meant that his tuition, housing, and meals would be paid for. He would have access to the fully equipped library and study with other great minds of his time. His parents did not have to worry about raising school fees anymore. He only had to raise money for clothes, exercise books, and transportation, which he could easily do with his holiday work.

The journey back home seemed short. He couldn't remember all the beautiful scenery: the rolling hills, the stretches of flat land, and the occasional farmer who would cross the road, guiding a large herd of cattle and causing the cars to stop. When the taxi arrived at his stage, he got off and rushed home. A good two-hour walk.

"I was admitted to the university," he told his parents when he got home. "I will go to university, and there are no school fees." He could barely contain his excitement. Francis was home early, which was a bit odd, except that he had also decided not to work as they waited for the return of their son. But Maanzi didn't spend too much time thinking about it.

His father was not one to display his emotion, but his face lit up with pride, as he simply said, "Thank you for taking away shame and disgrace from us. You have made us proud, and you have done well."

Grace could barely control her emotions; she said, "We can now go out and hold our heads high. Now even if you never set foot in the university, at least the whole village will forever know that you passed and qualified to join and you were admitted."

Trying to control her emotions, she changed the subject and asked, "Where will the money to transport you to university come from? You also need shoes; you cannot go to university barefooted! We have to start working hard." And on and on she went.

"We will figure it out; we usually do," Francis reassured his wife.

"We can sell the whole family land and only leave the piece where our house and plantation are if it comes to that," his father said, determined.

But Maanzi said, "Never again. Not this time." There were nine of them now, and his time was done. His siblings would need all the money their parents had. Since Uncle Jay had children of his own, it wasn't an option to send the children away to him (which Maanzi thought was a blessing in disguise, as children should not have to be separated from their parents).

He had mixed feelings as he walked to Zuri's home to tell her the news. He knew she would be excited for him since he had achieved what they both wanted to do, but he was also sad. They started together, they should be finishing this together. He was also worried about what would become of her after she had the baby. School was starting soon, and he wouldn't be there to help her.

Zuri was in the kitchen preparing dinner for the family.

"Hello there," Maanzi announced his coming.

Zuri, immediately put down the wooden ladle with which she was stirring beans in a cooking pot and turned slowly to face her friend as he stood in the doorway.

"Tell me, please tell me you made it," she said as she rushed toward the door to meet Maanzi.

"I made it," Maanzi replied.

"Silly, and why do you look like your cow just died?" Zuri said as her mouth was wide open. She hugged him and said, "I knew you would make it. That was our plan from the beginning. We wanted to be different, to make a difference in our lives," Zuri said with a hoarse voice and teary eyes. She was pleased with him.

Chapter 18

WHEN MAANZI LEFT HIS VILLAGE ON THE FIRST DAY THAT UNI-versity opened, much as he loved and cared deeply about his family, he had a feeling that it would be a long time before he would return. He had already decided that he would look for part-time jobs around the university to raise the money he would need to buy necessities, and if he was lucky, he would be able to save some money to help his father with his siblings' school fees.

University was like a dream. It was even larger than his former school and had people from everywhere. The majority of the students were from rich families and had been born and raised in the cities by educated parents. There were even people from other countries. The student accommodations were even better than he had expected, and the meals were great. A few people complained about the food, but he was happy that he was guaranteed two meals every day. While he didn't speak as fluently and eloquently as many of the students in his class, he soon realized that in this environment, what really mattered most was your performance in the classes, and that, he was good at. Great even. He found his niche among a group of Christian students who would meet once a week to pray and study the Bible together. These people formed the core of his friendships, and they would support each other in class as well, often studying together and pushing each other to excel.

At the end of the term, while many students went home, a few got menial jobs to raise money for their upkeep. Most of the students in the university were from middle-class families, and a few from high-class with their parents as ministers or ambassadors, so they did not have to work on holidays.

Maanzi was fortunate and got a job as a file clerk at a law firm that had recently been set up. Such jobs were usually for students who were enrolled in the Law courses and in the upper years of their study, who would have made such connections, but one of his new friends, who was in his final year, knew the people who were setting up the office and asked that he be given the job. They were setting up a full-service law firm, as was common in this place. He would soon realize that they dealt with all cases: commercial and corporate law, family disputes, international adoption, and employment law. His job may have been menial and his earnings meagre, but this was as good as it gets. It was not selling pancakes, it was an office job. And the best part was that soon, he would be in his clinical years and start to get work helping in hospitals instead.

He stayed with a distant relative since the university was closed during the holidays. He could not wait to get done with the basic sciences and start clinical rotations, see patients and 'save lives' as they all talked about the reason for being in medical school.

He looked longingly and yet enthusiastically as his senior colleagues wore white coats going to the hospital wards, as they, the first year medical students headed to the anatomy rooms where they were dissecting the human body and learning its functioning.

There are nights, especially towards the end of each term, that Maanzi and a few of his classmates would spend very many hours, deep into the night, pouring over the human cadavers, studying and cramming the names of the muscles of the upper limb, or the names and position of the cranial nerves. But this was no match for Maanzi's determination to excel and pass all his exams. He had dreamed of this moment, and it was here. He was in medical school, studying with the best minds of his generation and the children of the rich or educated parents. He was grateful for his parents, for their sacrifices. Some days, he would become emotional thinking about the journey. And when these demons threatened to overwhelm him, when he could not sleep, he sat in the lecture rooms for most of the night reading. It is all he needed and wanted to do, read. He did not have to worry about fees, food or accommodation, but to read, and he did. He began to excel and was among the students with good grades in his class.

Meanwhile, back in his village, it was time for Zuri to give birth. The poor girl had a protracted, difficult birth under the supervision of a traditional birth attendant (the same one who had helped her mother give birth to her). Her mother came to support her. It would be ten hours later that she would finally give birth. She was exhausted and could not believe the pain she had endured, but fortunately, her child was here and healthy. She cried immediately. It was a beautiful girl. She named her after her mother, Kesiime, and so gave her the name Kesi. It meant grateful, and she was so grateful that both she and her daughter had survived an ordeal that killed so many women in these parts.

A relative who was visiting the city relayed the news to Maanzi, and he found himself wishing that he could have been there to help her take care of her daughter, a real baby this time, and not a banana leaf doll.

"Have you heard the news yet?" the man from their village asked.

"What news, his heart almost skipping a beat, hoping nothing bad had happened to his friend," Maanzi asked.

"Your cousin Zuri had a baby girl. They are both okay. I saw her last week. I had gone over to see her father Jackson over some issues," he reported.

"Oh, thank goodness, all is okay," Maanzi was relieved.

Zuri had been forced to grow up so fast, fast enough to become a mother herself. In many ways, she was still a child, forced to raise another child. First, she was unable to afford the basic necessities herself, and now, she had a child but no support, no money, and no future.

It would be a year before Maanzi could afford to take a holiday but also gather just enough money to go home and see his parents, siblings and Zuri. They did not communicate at all; there were no phones, and Maanzi's parents did not come to the city to see him, for mostly financial reasons. He only hoped that Zuri was doing well with her baby.

At eleven months, Kesi had started to walk, though she fell after every few steps, but she never wanted any help standing back up. She seemed determined to get back up on her own. She could also say a few words. She looked healthy and well taken care of. Zuri was coming to terms with being a mother. She had faced the possibility that she may never get a chance to go back to school, finish college, and become a teacher.

Their days were mostly the same. She got up, fed her child as she also ate a light meal, and then had to help her mother with her chores just like before, only that when she went to fetch water, Zuri would carry her baby on the back. Initially, the villagers would taunt her and ridicule her, as some did not know that she had been pregnant.

"Look at her who for a time thought she was different from all the other girls," neighbours would say.

"Who is the baby's father?" some continued to wonder. "Or are they so many that you cannot choose one?"

"You who refused to get married early like the rest of us, saying that you wanted to study, we now see what you really wanted. You wanted to disgrace your parents and the girls in this village," other people said, but she persevered.

This was to be her life, and the faster she could adjust to it, the better.

She was grateful that for now, Kesi was still too young to understand what was being said. Eventually, this seemed to calm down, except for the occasional bully who would still taunt her every once in a while.

After one such incident, her mother walked into her room and found both Zuri and Kesi crying. Looking at her daughter and grandchild crying, Zuri's mother ran and embraced her daughter, ignoring the grandchild, who started crying aloud.

"Stop crying, Zuri, stop crying!" her mother begged.

"You are a woman now, and you have a child to take care of. Mothers don't have the luxury of just sitting there and crying. I wish I could take away your pain," she said over and over again, "but I can't.

Once the milk is spilled, it can never be recovered, so dry your tears and breastfeed your baby." Her mother admonished her.

"Mom, why did I have to think that I would be different? Why did you and my father fail to pay my school fees? Why couldn't we afford to buy books and uniforms? Why, why me?

Zuri continued to sob.

"Go away from me," she said, pushing Kesi away as she crawled to her feet.

"No, do not push your daughter that way; it's your baby," her mother said as she lovingly reached for Kesi.

"Why not? My daughter ruined my life. This pregnancy destroyed everything I dreamed of and aspired to become. I love children, but it was not yet time for me to get one, and this baby did not give me a fighting chance, Mom."

Zuri refused to be comforted. She was tired of everything and everyone and was taking it out on her child. Her mother was silent, understanding that she needed to vent yet not willing to let her off the hook.

After a while, she said, "This child needs to be fed," and then she handed Kesi to Zuri and walked away.

As days passed, Zuri resolved to move on with her life and make use of every opportunity that she had. She was tired of oscillating between self-pity and depression; neither were getting her anywhere.

Since she had always loved to teach, she started to teach the village kindergarten school at the same church grounds where both she and Maanzi had first gone to school. The kindergarten, by this time, had disintegrated and there were no children because they did not have a teacher. So, Zuri asked a few parents to give her their kids so that she could help them. She would get very little money that would help to buy soap and clothes for her daughter.

One afternoon as she came home from teaching the school, someone who looked familiar was sitting on a wooden stool under the tree in their compound.

"Hello, James, nice to see you again," she said, half hoping that he had come to his senses and was here to apologize and take her home with him.

"Hello, Zuri," James replied, with a cold demeanour.

"Have you seen Kesi? She has your eyes. Have you come to take us with you?"

"No, Zuri. I am here to see the girl, but I have no intention of taking either of you," James replied. "I have a wife now."

"Mister ... whatever your name is, you'd better leave before Mr. Wrath comes home," Zuri's mother told James. By Mr. Wrath, she meant Zuri's father, who would not be at all courteous to this man who had deceived his daughter and got her pregnant.

James stood up and walked away without even looking back.

Zuri ran into the kitchen and started to cry again.

"Why are you wasting your tears, my child?" Zuri's mother asked.

"I hoped that he had come back for Kesi and I. I hoped that if he saw his daughter, maybe he would change his mind."

"He is a married man, forget him and move on," her mother painfully concluded.

Zuri, of course, was outraged to see him again. Why in the world had he bothered to come? He was a painful reminder of mistakes and failed dreams that she was aware of every single day; she didn't need to be reminded of them. To vent, she decided to help her mother grind millet on the stone. Usually, she loathed the task, but today, she willingly volunteered. As her hand moved back and forth along the grinding stone, she spoke quietly.

"How could he show his face around here?" she repeated as she worked.

He who represented the thing that had killed her future changed her life and put her in a place that she now lived in, with no hope. She never wanted to see his face ever again, and her daughter would never know this evil monster who destroyed her mom's future (and perhaps her own). By the time she was done, the millet was as fine as if it had been ground at the mill. Her mother stared at the floor, grateful and then worried as if to ask if she was okay.

"Are you okay?" her mom asked.

"No, I am not, but I will be okay. I usually am. It is the only way," Zuri responded.

She wasn't, but she would be, and that's what mattered.

A few months later, when Maanzi came home to visit, he realized that her situation was getting dire. Where Zuri had always worn used clothes, this time her clothes were tattered and left her half exposed. Her hair was full of dirt, and she looked malnourished and depressed.

"When I finish school and start working, I will pay for your school fees if you still want to go back to school and pursue your teaching career," Maanzi told Zuri, trying to cheer her up. He could not afford to give her any money now, as he was barely making ends meet, especially since he was trying to help his parents by supporting his siblings and buy his own supplies for university.

"I would like that," Zuri replied, looking away from her cousin to hide the pain and the tears in her eyes.

She liked the idea of going back to school, though she thought to herself, *Will I last that long to go to school before I am married off?*

More and more, she realized that she was now a burden to her family since she and Kesi were two extra mouths to feed. She heard her father say that he would agree to marry her off, preferably as soon as possible, even if it meant sending her off for no dowry at all.

"I will come back next holiday and see you," Maanzi told his cousin, ever the hopeful one.

"Good-bye, my friend," Zuri replied, hugging her cousin and holding on a bit longer, wondering whether she would still be around the next time he came home.

"I do not know how much longer I can hold this together, but I will try," she told her friend.

Zuri's mom stood at the doorway to the kitchen and waved good-bye to Maanzi.

Chapter 19

WHILE MAANZI RETURNED TO THE CITY AND WORKED HARD AND studied hard, a cloud of change was looming over Zuri's head. There had been some suitors. She had pleaded with her mother against each of them, but the financial situation was dire. Jackson had been ill for two months, and they didn't have much money to take care of him, let alone her other siblings. Seeing the situation was only growing worse, and Kesi was getting older and that meant she needed more things to survive, she finally agreed to marry a man named John, who was a medium-built dark-haired guy, with a rough beard. He was in his late twenties.

John was from what would be considered a wealthy family in these parts. His family had plenty of cattle and a large piece of property. They lived five villages away from Zuri's parents' home. John had not had much schooling himself, so he had dropped out early. He had inherited a sizable piece of land and a few cows. When he was sober, he seemed docile and someone she could negotiate with. However, he was a man given to vices and so had a problem with alcohol and was a chain smoker, and for that reason, the girls in his village had avoided him.

But when he met Zuri, he treated her kinder than some of the people in the village. She knew that she was risking it if she married him since she had heard that he was involved in brawls at the local bars, but he had a bit of property and was not as poor as they were. Hopefully, she would be able to work hard in his plantation and raise enough money to sustain the family. Besides, he was one of the few younger ones, given that her previous suitors were older married men who were looking for a younger second or third wife.

Once the decision was made, the ceremonies were then carried out in a rush, and she quickly moved to his house.

One day, Maanzi was walking in the city, just outside the university gate. He heard a voice behind him calling, "Maanzi, how are you?" It was Joshua, a veterinary assistant from their village, who was in the city to buy supplies.

"Hello sir, how are you?" Maanzi replied as he walked toward him.

"I saw your parents last weekend," he said. "I was at your Uncle Jackson's home, attending his daughter Zuri's giveaway ceremony."

Maanzi's heart sunk, and his face showed. "What?" he asked. "To who? Why?"

Briefly, Joshua narrated the story to Maanzi. "Your cousin's giveaway was a very painful ceremony to watch," he said. "If anyone saw the tears and pleading of that young girl not to be given away and did not shed tears, then they are not human. Her father cried, and her uncle, your father, had to hand her over to the in-laws. Jackson loved his daughter like a son, and that's why he was keeping her in school.

"Anyhow, I will tell your parents that I saw you and that you are well. Good-bye." Joshua waved his hand at Maanzi, as he stood there, frozen in time.

The story sparked an unwanted image in Maanzi's mind of a village man who sells his goat to the butcher. As the goat is hauled away, it screams, but the owner has nothing to do; he has been paid, and there is no turning back. In many ways, Maanzi thought, that was the situation with Zuri. He imagined Zuri, with her baby on the back and a small bag of her belongings on her head, following John out of her father's home into the unknown future. He imagined Zuri crying out to her father, pleading to let her stay home. He imagined Zuri's mother hiding inside the house and groaning for her beloved lost daughter.

Within three months, Zuri came back to her parents' home. She had had it with John. She had tried to endure him. She knew that in this part of the world, men on occasion reached out and hit their wives. She wasn't naïve. She had heard of stories and seen some cases, and culture and society kept a blind eye on this. She also knew that if she went back home, her parents would tell her that she should endure, but this time, she was at her wits' end. She had taken to working in her new home. It was a lovely house, and her husband's plantation was larger than her parents'.

The other women in the compound had been suspicious of her in the first few months, but after they heard John beat her one time too often, their stares had turned to pity and tolerance, and so they began to sit and talk to her when her husband was away. The women now welcomed her as 'one of their own' she was sharing in their 'suffering'. It took a while for her to get used to being alone with Kesi in the evening since John was always at the bar deep into the night. It was awfully quiet, and she was afraid that someone would attack her in this new village.

Her new home was about five villages away from where her parents lived. The house was made of mud and wattle. The walls were brown. There were mud floors and a tin roof. The house had two bedrooms and a living room. The kitchen was in a shed behind the house, and just like her parents, she used firewood to cook the meals. The homestead housed two other brothers; they were also married, and each had children of their own. Their recently widowed mother lived in a house with two grandchildren (a boy and girl) from her daughters. The boy and girl were aged five and seven, respectively; they reminded Zuri of Maanzi and herself.

How she hoped that the world would be kinder to these two than it had been to her.

Her new home was nearer to the town, so there was easier access to shops (and bars). It was hilly, though, and it seemed like she had to climb up or go down a hill wherever she went, whether to the well, the shops, the village clinic, church, and so on.

She could have settled down faster, but John made this very difficult. He would argue and fight but was kind and apologetic in the mornings.

"Good morning, my wife. I really do not understand what came over me last night. I am very sorry, it will not happen again."

"You know I love you and only you," Zuri would say with a sad face.

"Why do you blame me for looking at other men?"

"I am sorry," John replied as he sat down on his stool to drink a cup of milk. He had hired a small boy from their village to take care of his few cows. In turn, this boy was allowed a cup of milk every morning to take to his family. After his breakfast, he went to the banana plantation and worked for one to two hours where he would cut down a bunch of bananas and carry them to a nearby bar, where he sold them and drank alcohol.

He came home late at night.

Singing drunken songs as he approached his house, he woke up the whole neighbourhood. Once he got home, he was very irritable, and any small thing caused him to hit her.

Bang, bang, bang. "Zuri, where are you? Open my door quickly, or I will break it open," he commanded.

Immediately Zuri opened the door, and he slapped her face.

"What took you so long? Are you sleeping before I come home? Lazy woman," he said as he staggered into his seat.

"Why is the food so cold?" John asked and kicked the plate away, scattering the food all over the ground. Zuri hid her face as he came over her and started to kick her and punch her head. And on and on. Somehow, there was something new each day. But the last straw was when he came home and woke Kesi up. In his anger, he had thrown a plate of hot food toward her daughter. "This food is so cold, not even fit for a dog," John yelled.

Fortunately, Zuri had been quick and diverted the plate before it reached the three-year-old. Kesi had cried uncontrollably, which had only served to incite his anger even further. But Zuri reached for her daughter, and they ran out of the house to the kitchen, where she consoled her. As he yelled from the living room, they heard John saying, "Will you stop that good-for-nothing child from shouting? Like mother like daughter."

Early the next morning, Zuri waited for John to leave home, and then she immediately packed their few belongings and took Kesi back home. Surely her mother would understand and provide refuge for them while they figured things out.

"I cannot go back to that man. He will kill me and my daughter," she cried when she first came back home.

Her mother had looked at her in the eyes and replied, "My daughter, you have to be strong to be a woman. You should not be coming here every time your husband lays hands on you."

She had expected that's what her mother would say. Still, she stayed quiet.

"Women get beaten by their husbands, but that's how marriage is. You have to stay there for your children," her mother admonished.

But fortunately, she allowed her to stay to recover. After one week, John came to Zuri's home to pick her up. It was mid-morning, but he was already staggering and reeked of alcohol. Whether he had taken the alcohol along his journey or perhaps that was from last night was anybody's guess. His eyes were red as pepper and seemed to be protruding from his head. He murmured a few incomprehensible words and struggled until he voiced out an incoherent apology.

"I am so sorry," he said. "I will not beat my wife again." His expression seemed detached from the words he was trying to say. Was he even sorry?

Zuri was determined not to return to that kind of suffering. She had tried her best and given it her all.

"I am not going back with you," she stated, standing behind her father.

"Well, then, I guess I will have to get my dowry back, so I can go get another wife for myself," John said. He knew her family's need was great, and with that blackmail, he would have her where he wanted her: at his house.

"Do you see what you are getting us into?" Jackson stated. "You will have to go back and do as he asks. If you were not very stubborn, you would not be provoking him to anger," he said.

She knew that he was not being mean. He was simply scared, and his next words confirmed that:

"We do not have the dowry to pay him back, so you have to go back."

Her brother had recently married, and the cattle they had gotten for Zuri's dowry had been given to his bride's family. It was a vicious cycle. But her father seemed set to bruise her.

"In fact, you are not welcome here anymore. Stay at your husband's home and be a submissive wife," he said.

Yet still, she pleaded, "Please, Dad. Please let me stay. He will kill me."

But his face seemed set, and there was no changing his mind once this was done. So on impulse, she pleaded, "Let my Kesi stay here with you then. I will go with him and will not come back to bother you," Zuri stated. "Promise me that my daughter will be safe."

She had that look in her eyes which spoke of resignation to her fate and yet an unspoken determination.

What was she determined to do?

In a rare move aimed to placate her, her father agreed. "Your daughter can stay," he said, as though to silently tell her that he knew what she suffered, was sorry he could not help her but would try with her child.

Zuri knew she was not wanted at her home. Though her parents still loved her, they had given her up. She was not welcome back home. This place was no longer her shelter. She realized at that moment that she would have to look out for herself. So, she resigned to her life of violence and abuse; she seemed to give up her fight. She would go back and work hard and learn to survive in his household. Maybe once she bore him children, he would be kinder. But in the meantime, at least Kesi would be safe.

Soon enough, she started to have children with John. She had been pregnant when she had run away from home but did not know it. But a few months later, she realized that she was pregnant again; six months later, she gave birth to another girl, and a year later, she gave birth to a boy.

Her children were her joy and sunshine. She carried them wherever she went. Where the birth of Kesi had been mired with sorrow, these children signified hope for her, hope that her marriage would become more tolerable. She was happy that she was no longer alone in the world. They healed a place in her heart where she previously had felt detached from connecting with anyone else because of the hurt she had experienced at the hands of her parents and her husband. For a while, she had also been a bit resentful, since Maanzi did not come to see her. She would hear stories that he was progressing and doing well in school, but he seemed to have forgotten her.

However, although the birth of her children reduced the physical and verbal abuse in her home, it did not stop, though she tried to shield her children from their father. The latest fight was because she had been seen talking to the brother of one of her new friends in the village. He was younger than she was and was home on holiday; when he saw her in the plantation, he had stopped to greet her, and they chatted for a while. One of John's brothers had passed by and seen them and then gone to John with the news.

"I will destroy this face you are so proud of," John taunted as he tried to scratch the side of her face; she tried to cover her face and fight him off. "And even if you leave me, no man would want to marry you, with your now ugly face."

He had managed to leave a few cuts.

"Don't even think of going out to the hospital," John continued. "I know you want to go around seeking sympathy. No one will sympathize with you, even your parents did not want you back."

Just when she thought she was immune, somehow, he still managed to break the fences she thought she had constructed to shield her damaged heart.

So, she stayed in her house and healed naturally. Even then, she would rise each morning to take care of her children's needs. They were all she had. They were an example of what was good and beautiful and innocent, and she would vow repeatedly to keep them that way as much as possible. They gave her hope and a reason to live. Her desire to protect them was so much greater than the desire to protect herself.

Marriage had grown her in ways she never knew were possible. She now understood the way of life. But she was grateful. Oh, the irony that the children she worked so hard to save were the ones who were saving her each day.

Some days, she would put her two children into bed, sit by herself and begin to wonder as she sobbed.

"How did I get here?"

"Why has the world been so cruel to me?"

"Should women not be allowed to dream?"

"Why did James really take advantage of me?"

"What was Maanzi doing?"

"This is my life now, I was a fool to think that I could rise above this."

Her thoughts would be interrupted by a cry of one of her babies.

Chapter 20

WHEN MAANZI JOINED THE CLINICAL YEARS OF MEDICAL SCHOOL, he gave up the clerical job and started to spend his holidays doing electives in rural hospitals, learning and honing his skills of history-taking and clinical examination of patients. Clinical rotations had a deep impact on him and informed the type of physician he wanted to be and later what specialty he wanted to pursue. In these hospitals, the administration would provide accommodation, food and a very small upkeep allowance, which Maanzi would save up to use during the school period, and once in a while sharing it with his siblings.

During one of his holidays, he volunteered in a refugee camp where he went with a classmate from his medical school year. The situation was dire. He saw children bearing children, severe malnutrition and human suffering that left him unsettled. But there was not much you could do in the refugee camp clinic, so all these patients were referred to the teaching hospital in the city. They would then be put in the United Nations (UN) vans and be driven to the hospital, many kilometres away.

Maanzi decided to try another rural hospital in the Eastern part of the country. Here, he was scarred as he witnessed how the lack of resources in rural hospitals affected the lives of the patients and especially the children. It was a malaria season, so many children were admitted with complicated malaria, but more disturbing at the time was that there was a shortage of blood in the hospital, district and country. The babies were dying on the wards, every day, there was a death from severe anemia. Desperate, Maanzi took to the hospital phones and started calling all around: district blood banks, regional blood banks and the national blood bank. The answer was the same, there was no blood, with a lot of explanations that did not make any sense at all.

One day, Maanzi hurried to the children's ward in the morning, only to find a mother getting her child from oxygen and putting it on her back and getting ready to head out of the hospital.

"What are you doing, where are you taking the baby?" Maanzi asked puzzled.

"We are taking the baby home," mother responded with a straight face.

"Why?" Maanzi asked.

The woman gave him a look of 'are you so naïve that I have to tell you what is going on?'

"Because my baby is going to die anyway. If he dies in the hospital, it is very expensive to transport a dead body home. We simply do not have that money. So, we will go home now, we can still take a public taxi and do not have to pay so much," the woman responded, and she was getting out of the door.

Maanzi was distraught and thought to himself, *this is wrong, and there I thought that I was finally ready to start saving lives.* The experience was painful, because he had lived this life, and he knew what it means to be out of options, to lack, and to feel helpless at times.

"This needs to change," he resolved. How? He did not yet know.

He continued to do electives every holiday until his fifth year of medical school.

One elective deserves mention. During his fourth year of medical school. He returned to the hospital where it all started.

The hospital in his mother's home district. The hospital where he had been sick as a child and could not see a doctor. The hospital where he had witnessed a child die while waiting to be seen and where the woman was being taken out of the hospital after dying in labour. He thought to himself *now that I have some knowledge and skills, I will go back to this hospital and help.*

Maanzi asked a friend to join him; he was in the same fourth year of medical school and also came from the neighbouring district where this hospital was found.

"Jack (not his real name), would you like to go with me for an elective in this hospital?"

"Sure," Jack replied.

"I wrote to the Medical Superintendent and he promised to give us accommodation and meals, so you and I will be pretty much running the hospital; think of how much hands-on we are going to get!" Maanzi continued.

"Count me in," Jack replied. Jack is now a specialized General Surgeon and a lecturer and he is a good one.

It had been at least fourteen years later after the day that had put Maanzi on the path of desiring to become a doctor. The situation was the same, there were only two doctors in this district hospital; the hospital lacked the basic supplies to treat emergencies or treat people with life-threatening yet treatable conditions such as women bleeding after giving birth, and babies with severe anemia from repeated malaria infections were dying and so were young adults from road traffic accidents.

"Hello, you are now working here, eeeeh? You are all grown up," one stranger approached Maanzi in the hallway of the hospital.

"I am your mother's cousin, and we have our mother down this way, please come and see her.

"We had heard that you two were coming since morning, but we have not seen you."

"My colleague and I will be shortly rounding on the inpatients after we finish the outpatient clinic here," Maanzi replied. "We will come to see you then."

"And we have not been able to buy the drugs the nurses told us to buy," he responded.

"Does the hospital have any, that you may help us with? We don't have any money to go out and buy from the private pharmacy," he continued.

At this conversation, Maanzi's anger burned up again, having been training in the government-run hospitals, with limited resources, and having to send relatives to buy drugs and supplies, even in emergencies, at the university, he had witnessed patients die before their relatives returned with the much-needed emergency supplies.

What could a poor medical student, who struggled to afford even his own books, toothpaste, and pens do? Maanzi was once again drowning in these thoughts and helpless situation.

He owned one shirt and one pair of trousers and only one pair of shoes. If he had not gotten a scholarship into the medical school, he probably would still have been on the streets selling pancakes. He felt outraged, and yet helpless.

"Things have not changed, not at all," he said out loud as he turned his face away from this stranger, who identified himself as his relative.

The memories of fourteen years prior, in that hospital, came back rushing like strong waves from hell into his mind, crushing his chest so that he struggled to get air to breath, choking him as he felt a lump at his throat, unable to find correct words to speak and paralyzing him with an overwhelming sense of resentment for the system that had failed so many poor people and continued to do so, and fearing that things may never change and that he was disillusioned thinking that he could make a difference in any way.

"Why do things never change?" he thought about how he had wanted to bring change so badly, and now in front of him were the reasons why people were still dying inside this hospital.

During their second day in the hospital, the two young and energetic medical students divided up the inpatient wards for the evening rounds. This allowed one of the doctors in the hospital to deal with the very sick patients as the students rounded on the inpatients, they would converge and discuss their patient management plans with him and go and implement them.

As Maanzi entered the nurses' room, he saw some of the patients' relatives carrying covered containers outside, going in groups.

"Why are these women carrying covered basins that smell so badly?" Maanzi asked one of the nurses.

"The toilets have not been flushing for some weeks now. There is no running water, so they are carrying the urine and feces from patients to the outside latrines," responded one of the nurses.

But at night, some of them empty the basins in the compound because they fear to walk in the dark. The outside latrines were quite far and there was no electricity in the hospital to give these poor women light out in the compound.

Maanzi then began to ask himself, "What was the real problem? Why is it that things had not changed, and people were still dying in this same hospital?"

He began to imagine how many more children and women had died in the years past and who would die in the years to come if nothing was really done to change the situation. How is it possible that a whole district hospital could run without running water and stable electricity for days, and this was acceptable by those who managed it? How was it acceptable to the community and the leaders of the district?

He often went and knocked on the administrator's door to seek answers which were never given, and there was always an impression that these hospital challenges were being handled at a higher level, and as hospital administrators, well, for them, their hands were tied, and they were waiting on someone higher in the food chain to provide the solutions. They knew what was wrong, but strangely, they could not do anything about it. The administrators were from around the hospital, some of them had even lost their own relatives in the same hospital and were quite close to the ailments that plagued health care that was being provided.

"Maybe, as a full doctor, after medical school, one may be able to make a difference. This was the only way to bring change, to advocate, to be involved in management, allocation of resources, and maybe, as a medical doctor, the leaders in hospital and the political arena would give someone an audience to discuss the plight of the patients." Maybe, was all Maanzi got out with from their four weeks of elective at this hospital. "The deaths, the suffering and the state of the healthcare offered to the patients, for some reason were worrying and as a medical student, no one seemed to listen or care about your opinion. Maybe, if I finish medical school and qualify as a doctor, then, maybe then, someone may listen to me." Maanzi convinced himself. They returned to Medical school and worked hard on their final year. They studied and prepared for their final exams.

Soon, Maanzi will be graduating from university. Funny how fast time went. It would have been five wonderful years, and all he would need would be to complete one more year on Junior internship, working under direct supervision of consultants, after which he would be an official junior doctor, out practicing on his own, out saving lives at last, or so he thought. He found time to go see his parents. He was able to afford this because, during his fourth year in medical school, he had found a clinic that was owned and run by a Midwife/Nurse, who had asked him and his colleagues to help in running it once weekly. They made some wages seeing patients and helping this Nurse in this rural town triage her patients and send those who were very sick to the nearby hospitals. Maanzi could afford to help his parents with some of his siblings' school needs. Things were looking up, and hope was in the air.

Maanzi entered Zuri's parents' kitchen; he looked at Kesi. She was a little more than four years old. He could not help but think of Zuri. After talking to Kesi for a while, with his eye still on her, he greeted Zuri's mom. And continued to ask her; "How is Zuri doing?"

Because she had not heard what he had said, Kesiime, Zuri's mother, asked, "Were you talking to Kesi?"

Maanzi smiled. "Yes, as a matter of fact, I was," he said. "Isn't she a beauty?"

"Yes, she is. Just like her mother," Kesiime added quietly. "Come on in and have a seat," she said a bit louder, and Maanzi reached for a wooden stool, dusted it with his hands, and sat on it.

Maanzi and Kesiime had a long chat about how unfair life and family had been to Zuri, and then they talked about life in general.

Soon she changed the subject. "Now you have become Mr. Smarty Pants, right?" she joked. You really made it and you will soon become a doctor. "Dreams really come true, don't they?" Kesiime said.

Then as though she had mulled over this question for a while, she asked, "Do you think that going to school changes our culture and practices?"

Maanzi was not quite sure where she was leading with this question, so he kept silent. Fortunately, she seemed to be on a roll.

"Zuri should not have listened to you in the first place. She listened to you talking about going to school, changing your life and all. She truly believed that she could also study and become a teacher and become independent and escape the life of suffering."

Did she blame him for what had happened to her daughter? Maanzi was confused. If he had had his way, Zuri would not be in her current situation. But somehow, it was his fault that she was, and this was news to him.

"Why did she even begin to believe that was possible?" Zuri's mother said. "I was such a fool. I even supported those lofty dreams."

Ah! The crux of the matter. She blamed herself, and now she wanted to blame Maanzi as well for what had happened.

"But it is possible," Maanzi insisted. He had to, if only because Kesi's chances of getting an education depended on it. "I have seen women who are teachers. Even some of the teachers in university were women. More than half of my class are women, in fact, they do perform far better than we men do," Maanzi narrated.

But Kesiime was unaffected by what Maanzi had just said.

"For the moment, when I realized her determination to study and her love for teaching, I dared to believe that life would be different for her. But no, we were dreaming. That's all it was: dreams that seemed so real, but soon you wake up and realize that's all it was. Just a dream. Women are meant to just have babies, farm the gardens, and look after their husbands. To dream bigger than that is to attract disappointment," Kesiime concluded.

She seemed to be unaware of her surroundings and continued, "my daughter reminded me of my young self. You know, for a time, I also believed that I could go to school and have an education. I fought my parents for a while, demanding that they allow me to go to school, but when my mother died, all that ended as well. My father did not see the point. I guess I desperately wanted my girl Zuri to have that chance if I could give it to her. Oh well, enough of this lamenting nonsense," she said as she rose from her stool.

Reaching out and removing the lid from a boiling pot of beans to check if they were ready, Zuri's mother continued. This time, she didn't look at Maanzi.

"I have not seen my daughter for a while," she said. "The last time she was here, she had bruises over her face, back, and arms; she looked unwell, tired, and ready to drop. But her father and I had to send her back, even when she pleaded with us not to.

"I worried that John was not kind to her. I heard that he had recently sold a portion of their land, and given his drinking habits, I don't think she received any money from him to help take care of the home. She works in the plantation and sells off some of the produce so that she has money to look after herself and her children, yet he is always accusing her of being stubborn and lazy. Stubborn because she refuses to give him the small money from the sale of her produce to buy alcohol and cigarettes.

"She has to be strong for the kids," Kesiime said.

Clearly, she was at a loss over what to do for her child. Both parents had given the advice they had received from their parents when they left their homes for their marriages.

"You go back." They had said to their once beloved daughter. But somehow, that did not relieve them; instead, it brought them untold pain and worry, and Kesiime fretted over changing her decision.

Seeing that the old woman was ageing over worrying about her child, Maanzi said, "I will go and visit Zuri on the weekend."

Maybe if he saw and talked to her, he would come back with a report that would relieve them all.

That Saturday, Maanzi borrowed a bicycle from Joseph's father and rode the distance to go visit Zuri. He had not seen her in the four years she had been married. But she saw him from a distance as she looked up from grinding her millet. He was pushing a bicycle up the bushy path to her house. Wondering whether her eyes were deceiving her, she rushed to where he was; realizing who he was, she embraced him.

Zuri stood still for a moment, looking at her cousin and friend. He was different: well dressed, groomed, and healthy-looking.

On the other hand, Maanzi barely recognized the woman he was looking at. She was thin and wore old clothes, with an exhausted look. She had so many scars, old, healing, and fresh ones, and they seemed to be everywhere: her face, neck, and arms.

Maanzi put the bicycle against the wall of the house and quickly came to embrace his cousin.

"I am so happy to see you, Doctor Maanzi," she said, her joy was evident as she held onto him for a while. She would not cry, although she was close to tears. Happy tears, but she resolved she would not cry as she hugged him.

"No, not yet. I am still a medical student, but soon I will be a doctor" Maanzi responded.

There was silence.

But as he stared at her, silently appraising her, she felt the urge to explain.

"I gave up my dream. My life ended," she said as she pulled herself away from him and walked toward her house.

Maanzi was battling with so many feelings; they were threatening to explode if he wasn't careful.

"I am glad you are here," Zuri said. "I am happy you came. Have you seen my daughter, Kesi?" she asked.

He nodded in reply as she seated him in their small living room.

"How is she?

Is she well?" she asked, anxious to hear about what had become of her child.

"I worry about her, you know." This time, there were tears.

She pointed at the children sitting on the floor playing and said, 'This is Jill, Joy, and Jade, my children. Jill is three, Joy is two, and Jade is one. I am expecting another one."

"What?" Maanzi asked, surprised.

"Yes, I am expecting another baby soon," Zuri repeated as she sneezed and wiped her tears. "What does one do if they are not in school, not teaching or doing anything better with their lives? A wife is meant to produce children, right?"

Zuri tried to fight her tears back. Maanzi was outraged, looked sad and distraught, with no words to express his feelings.

Realizing that this was hurting more than helping, Zuri said, "This is my life now. I have accepted it and have learned to survive. I gave up my childhood fantasies. Those were not for me, I guess. Now I have children to raise and protect."

Maanzi looked up, only to realize she had been talking to him. "Look at you. You look very distinguished, all grown up and all," Zuri said with a genuine smile. She truly was happy for him. "Tell me all about university and your new life. Where do you go from here?"

So Maanzi told her everything, about his holiday jobs, the new friends, and the people in the village and what they were up to. He told Zuri that he was planning to advocate for women and children as he starts to work, and hopeful that he could save one life at a time. He told Zuri that he had met many other girls in hospitals who had been victims of rape, forced marriages, domestic violence, and women dying during pregnancy and childbirth. This was distressing to him and he hoped to find a way of speaking up and finding some solutions.

"I had hoped that I could contribute to your school fees when I start working so that you could continue school," Maanzi said. He had to broach the topic one last time. He knew that it wasn't culturally acceptable for him to pay school fees for her when she was the responsibility of her husband. Her mother had told him not to interfere, but he had to ask, if only to at least try and give her a way out of this place. She was his friend, they had dreamed about the possibilities of education together from the beginning.

Zuri looked away and said, "Forget about me, this is now my life. I guess it's not a woman's place to dream and aspire for better things. At least not for me."

He was a doctor to be, he had learned how to approach sensitive topics and there were so many arguments at the tip of his tongue fighting for release, but he also knew that now was not the time. It would only hurt and not help her. She had endured the shame of having a child out of wedlock with an unknown father, and she was living in a violent marriage, but asking her to leave her husband was something she should not be enticed into. There was ridicule to endure if that happened, so she needed to come to that decision. But he needed her to know that if ever she wanted to, he could help.

There was a long pause, and then came the question: "Will you take care of my daughter for me?"

He knew what she was asking. She needed him to follow through with her daughter Kesi. She was still young, and there was hope for her. She was at her parents' home, but she didn't know if they would allow him to take Kesi to school, given Zuri's own history. But she knew Maanzi would try. He had to.

Maanzi looked at her and nodded, and then he mouthed a silent yes. If only to repay the little girl for the wrong that her mother had endured at the hands of everyone else. But even while he promised, he knew that there would be hoops to jump. Zuri's parents were the primary custodians of Kesi, and they would not appreciate any interference on his part. But he hoped it would not come to that.

"I have no doubt you will do well," Zuri said. She was talking about his work. But he understood that she needed him to take care of her child, as that was all that mattered to her now.

It was approaching evening, and Maanzi had to start riding back home. They said their good-byes and wished each other well. As Maanzi rode away, Zuri wished that she was going with him.

But that was foolish; she rebuked herself as she rushed to prepare supper, bathe her babies, and put them in bed before John came home. Of late, he had started to yell at the children, so she did everything to ensure that they were out of his way when he came home. In the mornings, when he was a little more lucid, he would try to play with them, and once, he even tried to hold little Jade. But the little boy wailed on the top of his lungs, and John had to put him down. Then he yelled at her for inciting the children against him. It was endless, she thought to herself as she consoled her baby.

Today, he asked for his children as he settled down to eat. "Where are your useless children?" he asked. "Are they hiding under their beds? Come out here and greet your father!" he yelled while facing their room. He was staggering, and he almost missed a step, Zuri rushed to his rescue and steadied him.

However, the children did not come. Whether it was because they were afraid or because they were sleeping was anybody's guess, though Zuri thought it was the former. They were terrified of their father. But he didn't go to their rooms to find out, and for that she was grateful.

Chapter 21

MAANZI RETURNED TO THE UNIVERSITY AND WAS CONCENTRATing on his fifth year of Medical school. Final exams would be coming soon, and he did not want to fail any of his papers.

Meanwhile, Maanzi was in the study and carrying out clinical duties as a senior medical student. He was becoming confident with his clinical skills, and they would help the Junior doctor to do the majority of the work such as taking a history, examination of patients, drawing blood samples, going to the laboratory and doing blood grouping and crossmatching. Yes, at the end of the day, the final year medical students, felt like they were getting ready to become real doctors.

One Saturday afternoon, Maanzi was not on call in the hospital, so he had been resting in his room on the fourth floor of one of the men's residential flats. He was taking the much-needed rest before getting back to the library. There was a light tap on his door and one of the students entered and announced, "Maanzi, there's someone outside downstairs to see you. He said that it was very important and that he comes from your village."

"Oh, okay, I will be right outside with him," Maanzi replied. Wondering whether anything had happened to any of the people he loved. He dressed up, rushed to the bathroom, washed his face and headed downstairs and out.

Shock in his eyes, as the man standing before him, was he that had eaten his pancakes, humiliated him and refused to pay. Before him, was the man from his village who had ridiculed him those years ago for daring to dream of becoming a doctor.

"Oh, I hear you want to become a doctor, why don't you examine me and see if really I have ever eaten any pancakes," he had humiliated him.

"Good afternoon sir," he said; his fingers were nervously fidgeting with his torn hat as Maanzi looked at him with an expressionless face.

"My name is George."

"Hello, Mr. George," Maanzi said.

"Is everyone at home well?" Maanzi asked as he invited him to come into the common room and sit down on the sofa.

The man sat down, looking a little uneasy, but perhaps unaware of the label he was wearing on his forehead and what memories he brought back to his host. There were a number of things he could say to this man, but they all lay lodged in Maanzi's throat. Maybe he simply should take guilty pleasure in the fact that this man now needed his help.

"How is home?" Maanzi asked again. "What can I do for you today?"

"My son is very sick, he has no blood. I need your help," the gentleman began. He is in the children's ward and there is a long line of other sick children waiting to be seen. We have been there for a while now."

"Oh, alright, let me go upstairs, get my Clinical coat and we shall be on our way."

"Thank you, sir," the gentleman, looking weary, responded.

Maanzi raced up the stairs, put on his clinical coat, and stethoscope and headed out. The gentleman was standing by the doorway and Maanzi led the way to the hospital. The hospital was just a few meters away. The gates between the hospital and medical school were always closed and guarded by security personnel, but this weekend afternoon, the gates were ajar. The two men squeezed into the hospital from the university. Soon they were at the children's ward and the gentleman quickly pointed at his son who was in the attendance of his wife.

"That is my son over there," he pointed.

His wife raised her eyes and said hello to Maanzi.

"We were sent from our village health unit," she said. "They told us that he is very anemic and needs blood, but they do not have blood there, so they sent us here."

The gentleman jumped in to say that they had been referred two days prior, but because of lack of funds, they had waited at home in order for him to raise the transport they needed.

"Hi, would you like a hand with some of these sick children?" Maanzi asked his classmate who was on call with the Junior Doctor.

"That would be appreciated greatly," his classmate responded.

So Maanzi jumped into action. He drew blood from the very sick and almost paper white child, who was almost two years old. The baby was so lethargic that he did not even respond to the needle as he drew blood from him. He then rushed this blood to the lab, performed group, screen and crossmatching, and was lucky to find a matching blood type in the blood bank.

He returned minutes later with some blood and put it up on the child, in its mother's hands. There was no bed space left, and those discharged were slowly making their way out. Maanzi stayed with this couple until the first unit was over and he hung up the second unit. As the second unit was getting done, the child began to move all its limbs and talk to the mother. The father had a look of relief on his face.

"Momma, I want to eat," the child whispered.

Maanzi had a smile on his face. He filled up all the paperwork and handed over to the person on call.

He said goodbye for now.

"I will come back and see you tomorrow, but if you need anything, you know where I live."

"Thank you, thank you, thank you," the man kept repeating this over and over again.

"You are welcome," was all Maanzi could say. He was truly happy that he could actually be in a position to help this man and his son.

The next day, he rushed to the hospital and found the small boy feeding and feeling well. He was very pleased with the progress.

The gentleman had gone out to buy some food, but his wife was full of gratefulness for Maanzi.

"They told us that if he continues to do well, they will discharge us tomorrow," she announced.

"That's great if you go before I can see you again, safe travels and greet people in the village for me," Maanzi bid her farewell. As he left heading back to his residence, he realized what freedom forgiveness brings into a life. He was no longer holding anger against the gentleman for eating his pancakes and refusing to pay him, and for humiliating him many years prior. He was in charge of his destiny, his life had changed, and as his father and Uncle Jay had told him, he was practicing being kind and compassionate to people. He felt relieved and good. He was becoming a different man, a man that his father had always wanted him to be. He was in charge of his life now; he even had something to offer those who once thought he was a nuisance.

Maanzi could not wait to tell his parents about this encounter. When he finally got a chance to go home, he told his father first and then his mother.

"I do not even think this man remembered me," Maanzi said to Francis.

"No, I do not think he does," his father said. "That is why we should not waste our energy holding on to anger or thinking about those that hurt us. Most times they forget what they have done and move on, while you remain in bondage to them. I am proud of you; may God continue to bless you, my son."

But no, Maanzi did not have to talk about this incident to anyone from his village. The rumour mill in the village had spread the good news. Once they got home, George and his wife told everyone how Maanzi had helped them.

"Maanzi saved our son's life," George and his wife spread this good news in the entire village for whoever would care to listen. More and more people in this village were now struggling to send their children to school; they had seen the possibilities of what happened after educating a child. More and more parents found it acceptable to sell off a few goats and hens for the purpose of raising school fees without fear of ridicule from their peers, and in fact, some brave ones started to sell off pieces of their land. Their part of inheritance should be the investment in their education.

Life has a way of rewarding us for our deeds. And God has a sense of humour.

Just a few months after Maanzi had helped George with his son, and after the news had spread in the entire village that 'their village son' was indeed a doctor now. Those who made it to the city or happened to be in this teaching hospital made an effort to look for Maanzi, he was grateful for this because he got to hear news from home and know how his parents, siblings and grandparents were doing.

His roommate returned from the hospital and told Maanzi, "There is a woman outside looking for you. She says that she is your relative from your village."

Maanzi headed out and found a middle-aged woman with a very worried look on her face pacing back and forth outside his residence.

Immediately she saw him emerging from the hostel, she quickly moved toward him and greeted him.

"Hello Maanzi, how are you doing?"

"Hello, how are you doing? Is all well?" He asked.

"My son has been involved in an accident and he is here in the emergency trauma room. I wanted to come and get you for help," she reported, nervous.

"Sure, let me get my coat and stethoscope and I will come with you.

"Thank you, my son,"

Soon they were in the emergency trauma room. Maanzi helped to mobilize the needed supplies and take care of the boy.

The boy was the son of the man who had thrown Maanzi off his bicycle many years prior. The gentleman who had insulted him for wanting to get a ride with him on his bicycle. The same man, who had insulted Maanzi's father and called him useless for wasting money on school fees instead of buying a bicycle.

Yes, he was the same man, now standing in front of Maanzi, showing gratitude.

"We are very grateful, we cannot repay you for this," he said.

"You have done us all proud. I will let your father know about this," he concluded.

When the boy was well taken care of, Maanzi said his farewells and headed back to the university to study.

Maanzi wondered if this man remembered what he had done to him those many years ago. But it did not matter anymore.

Maanzi completed the university and passed his final exams.

He headed to the southwestern part of the country to do his Internship. He was very excited and yet enthusiastic about the opportunities for saving lives and changing lives.

But first thing's first. He was not going to waste any more time. He saved up his wages for the first few months and as the year was rolling by, he was going to make good his promises. Maanzi was thrilled to finally be able to buy back the land that had been sold in order for him to go to the fancy secondary school. He used a big portion of this money to buy the land and put a few cows there for his father to gain back his status in the village, but realistically, the cows were for emergency funds, school fees for the young siblings and any medical needs.

Jackson, Zuri's father and Maanzi's uncle, was on his way home from the shops one evening. "So, we hear Francis's son bought that land back?" a fellow villager asked.

"Yeah, he did. He bought the whole piece of land, in fact, and he has also put some cows on it," Jackson replied. "He is the first child to buy land for his parents. Let's face it, all of us were given land by our parents and have never bought any piece of land with our own earnings."

"Ah, I see. Now I know the reason why you were also trying hard to take your daughter to school," said the gentleman.

This comment made Jackson unhappy. It reminded him of his daughter's pain.

"This education thing should be looked at again and should not be ridiculed."

"His father is a happy man. His son has made him happy and took away his shame," Jackson concluded.

Maanzi's father had been ridiculed by the villagers and had not been allowed to give his opinion in any gathering because the men considered him a fool for selling his possessions to educate his son. Now, however, he was taken seriously by many in the village. He was invited to attend village meetings, his opinion on a contentious issue was sought, and when he stood to speak, many listened. They were curious to learn how a single man had defied the odds to educate a son who was now able to buy land for him and help him in educating his other children.

Maanzi's mother also found honour among the women in the village; she was given the audience in the women groups and was allowed to have a say in the Mother's Union Club, where before, she was not very welcome. How could a woman who was spending her life making pancakes to send her son to school have anything to offer? She was also considered a rebel since she was allowing her daughters to go to school and had advised her husband to sell land to take Maanzi to school. Women were supposed to listen to their husbands, not advise them. Maanzi's father was even asked to be the treasurer of the local church; they trusted that he knew how to be a good steward of finances. Maanzi's success in school was opening doors for his parents and siblings and serving to challenge and change perceptions in his village and beyond. People were beginning to question the status quo and realize that it was possible to have something better than what they had.

Chapter 22

WHILE MAANZI WAS AWAY WORKING AS A JUNIOR DOCTOR IN THE western part of the country, where he had spent most of his holidays as a medical student, life with Zuri and Kesi was turning a corner for the worst.

Jude, a distant uncle, said that he would like to take Kesi to live at his house with his wife and children. Jude and his family lived in a different district, had visited Zuri's parents, and learned about her from them. Jackson also confided that he was struggling to support her. She was now ten years with two more years in primary school, and while the government was providing some support for primary school students now, it was still difficult. Jude decided to take Kesi to his house. He asked Zuri's parents to pass on a message to Zuri that he would take good care of her daughter and would see her through school. Maanzi had lost the battle to take Kesi on. He lived by himself; money wasn't the only thing a child needed, as Jude was quick to point out. Many considered Jude, who was Jackson's cousin, as a more appropriate guardian than Maanzi, a young man with no wife and no life experience. Jude could be trusted with responsibility.

"You don't even have food in your house, and you live alone" Jackson had responded to Manzi's attempts at taking Kesi with him to the place where he lived and worked as a Junior Doctor.

"I promised her mom that I would take care of her," Maanzi had begged.

A decision has been made already; Kesi will go with my Cousin Jade. Jackson said as he walked away from Maanzi.

"See, you just came home today, after many months, and you seem to think that you know what goes on here," Jackson reprimanded Maanzi as he walked away.

Maanzi learned later that indeed Kesi had gone to live with Jude. He asked how she was doing, and Zuri's parents told him that Kesi was well looked after and that she had settled in well. Jude treated her as one of his own, they said. He was skeptical but hoped that he would be proven wrong.

But two years later, history seemed to be repeating itself. They had seen this scenario played out over and over again; why Maanzi allowed for it to happen on his watch was something that he would take a long time to forgive himself for. Uncle Jude had just given away his oldest daughter, who was in her mid-teens, for marriage and had received a few cows.

Kesi had only recently completed primary school and was determined to pursue secondary school. Whether Jude could not afford to raise the school fees or perhaps did not see the reason for sending her to secondary school was anyone's guess. He had just given out his own daughter into marriage, so he probably did not understand why Kesi still wanted to pursue secondary school. Since his daughter had not fought him over it, he didn't see why this had become an issue with Kesi.

Knowing that if he told Zuri she would want her daughter back, Jude set out to find Kesi's father. After he got the details about James, Jude got in touch with him and guilt-tripped him by saying that his child had nowhere else to live. He asked that he come pick his daughter so that he could support her wishes to study in secondary school, and he wanted to make sure James "thanked" him for looking after her. (That meant a monetary thank-you.)

Why Maanzi was never asked if he would at least support Kesi with school fees as she continued to live with Uncle Jude, was another question that no one would ever answer. Why would Jude go around looking for a father that has never wanted to be involved in his daughter's life since she was conceived? What made him think that James, who had made it clear that he did not want anything to do with Zuri and her daughter would welcome her now? And not to ask Zuri about her wishes for her daughter, well, Zuri was just but a woman, women were not privileged to make such decisions; decisions about their bodies, when to get married, whom to get married to, how many children to give birth to, and yes, even worse, who was to take care of their children.

In a strange turn of events, James agreed to take Kesi. No one knew why he wanted to be involved in her life when he had shunned her before this.

"Kesi, this is your father," Jude said to a stunned Kesi.

"Father? I have never been told about a father and have never seen him before," Kesi responded.

He was handsome, and she had the shape of his face. She could see the resemblance. She waited for a fondness to develop for him, but for the life of her, there wasn't any. Not now at least. There was still too much to resolve with this man.

"Since you really want to go to secondary school, you will go with him. He will take care of you from now on. He is your father," she heard her great-uncle Jude say.

She didn't have the time to digest what was happening before she was on her way with a stranger. *There is never any time to put down roots anywhere in my life*, she thought to herself as she walked to the bus stop with James, not quite comprehending what was happening. The questions were many, but she dared not begin to ask them. She had been taught to be a good girl, not to ask or talk back to your elders, to wait until you are talked to, and if something confused you, you had to give it time and figure it out yourself. How she hoped she would be given the opportunity to go to secondary school.

I am just doing this for an opportunity to go to secondary school, Kesi told herself.

If I have to live with a stranger in order for that to happen, I will do it, she was convincing herself that the decision taken by her great Uncle Jude, may after all not be a foolish one. He was hopeful for a chance at education. She was hopeful about life.

James had a wife and four children of his own, all younger than Kesi. Her excitement about getting a chance to go to a secondary school and have a happy life faded as fast as it had come when her stepmother gave her an icy welcome into the home.

In the few months she lived there, she would learn the meaning of fatigue as she had never known before. She was expected to help care for her half brothers and sisters, do laundry, and cook meals all the while going to school and doing work that was expected of her. She lost a tremendous amount of weight and walked around looking lifeless. This was not how it was supposed to be.

She vowed to hang in there until her first year of secondary school was done, and then she could escape to Jude's or her grandparents' home. Maybe she could enroll in another school. They would understand if she told them.

They had mostly treated her kindly. So early one morning, she managed to walk to the road and then get onto a Matatu and went to Jude's home. The journey was but a blur.

But Jude would not agree to have her hide in his home. The next morning, he went to the trading center and called James on the payphone. He told him that his daughter was at his house in case he needed to know of her whereabouts.

"I hope you will send back my daughter soon enough," James replied when he was told where Kesi was. "If she wants to continue school, she will have to earn the school fees."

"She is such a lazy girl, that one," James told Great Uncle Jude.

"You should go back to your father tomorrow if you want to continue school," Jude told Kesi.

"Where is my mother? I want to go back to my mother!" Kesi cried. "My mother would not treat me as that woman treats me."

"Trust me, Kesi, you should be going back to your father's home tomorrow. I will take you there myself and make sure that you arrive. I do not want any troubles with him," Jude said as he walked out of the kitchen and went to bed.

There has to be another way out, Kesi thought. She stayed up that night, desperately trying to think of another option. Early in the morning, in desperation, Kesi fled Jude's house and took another Matatu. It was a free ride for part of the distance. She did not have the fare, but she had begged the driver. She then walked the rest of the journey to her grandparents' home. She told them her story, and they seemed surprised.

"Aaaaah, Cousin Jude would not do that," Jackson said.

"But you do not understand. I do not even know that he is my father. How could he possibly treat his child like that?" Kesi said. "I am not going back.

"I will stay here," she continued. "I will give up school, but I can never go back there." She was determined. In many ways, her determination came through like her mother's.

Kesiime looked at her grandchild and saw her daughter's determination; this was all painful to her. She felt helpless as she watched her daughter and now her granddaughter in desperation to obtain an education, in search of a better life and future, and yet, she was not able to help them.

Soon or later, this little one will also realize that education is not for girls, she will give up like all of us, Zuri's mum thought to herself, watching her granddaughter sob and refuse to go back to her father.

"You go to bed, we will think about this tomorrow," her grandmother advised her.

"Why did my mother not come for me?"

"Did she even know that I was taken to live with this man called James?" Kesi asked her grandmother.

The things I could tell you little one, the horrors that I hope you never face, and your mother, my daughter! How I wish that she had not been a dreamer, she would never have been disappointed. I hope that you will not learn this the hard way, Kesiime was thinking to herself and then said to her granddaughter, "come here," and she hugged her whispering, "It will be okay."

Chapter 23

WHILE MAANZI CONTINUED TO IMMERSE HIMSELF IN THE HOSPI-
tal work, always wanting to treat every patient like he would want
his own mother to be treated and helping his parents pay for his
siblings' tuition fees, he was seemingly slacking at the one thing
Zuri had tasked him with. He still had not been able to get to help
or look out for Kesi, his friend's daughter, his friend's deep request.

Another life-changing event was about to happen in his life.
One that would bring him pain, but also more resolve. Funny how
people say 'what does not kill you, makes you stronger'.

Late one night, Maanzi's cell phone rang from the curtain box,
very high up towards the ceiling, where it was strapped with an
adhesive tape, lest it moves, and the reception disappears. This was
the only point in his hospital house where phone reception could
be got, so even when it was a cell phone, in many ways, it was
like a 'wall' line phone. Maanzi had just entered his house towards
morning from the operating room to rest a bit after a very long day
and night.

"Ring, ring, ring, ring," the phone kept going and going but he
was too exhausted and thought that it was maybe a dream at first.

He then jumped out of bed, climbed on the bed's headboard,
tiptoeing and balancing on his toes, he placed the answer button
and hung onto the window speaking into the phone. The voice

on the other side was his maternal uncle, his voice cracking and chocking intermittently, he informed him that his aunt had died in childbirth after two days in the hospital.

"Hello," his uncle called.

"Hello, it's too late in the night, is everything alright?" Maanzi responded.

"No, ah, um, your aunt has died giving birth," he answered.

Dead silence; Maanzi was shocked, angry, confused.

"Hello... hello... hello...," his uncle repeatedly called, his voice sounding like a bad dream, a nightmare of sorts.

Then Maanzi asked with a lump in his throat, "Whom one?" an answer he already knew but did not want to believe because he had known that his beloved aunt had been pregnant with her second baby. She had had a difficult first delivery and had fortunately accessed a cesarean section that had saved her and her baby boy.

And then the name came, the name that Maanzi did not want to hear. And wave after wave of ill emotions came crashing down on him like a hurricane or like demons which had been sent right from hell.

Whaaaat? Why? Maanzi was asking, disoriented. He had been spending his days, every day, saving women and their babies in this part of the country that he worked at, pouring out his spirit and soul into his work.

Since that day as a child, with his aunt in hospital, all Maanzi had done with his life was to try and prevent death, and now his passion was to prevent maternal and child death and his aunt was dead?!

"This cannot be happening," Maanzi mourned

His sleep and fatigue vanished so fast like morning fog before a rising summer sun.

"Why did she not get operated early? We knew she would not deliver naturally," Maanzi was sounding impatient with his uncle.

His uncle gave a long explanation that was incoherent through bursts of anger and tears.

Maanzi had seen so many women dying that he could guess what had happened to his aunt. He had also seen the horrors in the faces of all his dead patients' relatives as they usually stood helpless and angry to recognize why his uncle was speaking and behaving the way he did over the phone that night. He later asked his colleague who attended to her what had happened, the answer was that she died of a ruptured uterus and severe bleeding. The baby was salvaged alive but weak and would die a few days later. At operation, she had lost so much blood, but there was no blood in the hospital to transfuse her, so she never got out of the operating room. It had taken so much time to organize the needed supplies to do the surgery as well.

Maanzi was in another hospital, awake, saving lives almost 200km away from his aunt's home. Far from this hospital, where he first witnessed a maternal death, the same hospital where his aunt had taken him for treatment, many years prior. The memories were unkind and fresh.

This was almost twenty years ago when Maanzi had been in the same hospital with his aunt attending to him, it was twenty years after they had seen that family crying and carrying their dead young woman out of the hospital, at that age, Maanzi wondered what the family felt, but now it was his aunt, his childhood caretaker. She was dead, soon followed by second son. She had simply become an addition to the maternal and child death statistics, but he knew her name, he knew her love, he knew the care she gave him growing up, and he understood what that loss would mean. It's a loss that further changed his life forever.

"Alright, I will get onto the bus tomorrow morning," Maanzi told his uncle on the phone and hung up. He could not go back to sleep.

The next morning Maanzi travelled by bus almost 200km to go and attend the burial.

He arrived later in the afternoon at his grandparent's home, only to find that they had just finished burying her. He remembers a feeling of anger rising, angry at himself, "maybe if I was here, I could have saved her life," he thought. Or if they had called him the previous day, and so many 'ifs' were running through his mind. But it would not have taken more than one doctor to perform the life-saving procedure she needed if the necessary supplies and equipment were available at the hospital to save her life. In fact, the doctor who attended to her was more than 5 years Maanzi's senior and so he did not lack any skills to save her and her unborn baby. The hospital simply lacked basic supplies to save a woman in labour. Just like those many years ago.

His grandmother greeted him; "Hello Maanzi, you are welcome." And then gave she gave him what he had dreaded would be the response of most of the people at the burial. As he sat on a round wooden stool, head in his hands, eyes fixed to the ground, his mother Grace came in, gave him a hug, and cried. "Mercy (aunt Mercy, not her real name) cried and asked about you as she was being taken to the operating room, she wanted us to tell you…" Maanzi broke down crying out aloud.

His grandmother interrupted, "Stop that nonsense, your aunt is not coming back!"

When he had dried his tears, and looked up, his eyes met his grandmother's gaze, as she sat among other older women in from the village.

She then looked at Maanzi and stated, "Listen,"

She narrated a story of how his aunt spent nights awake when he had been sick with fevers together with her other sisters, how she carried him to hospital on her back many times, and how she had died giving birth while she had heard that Maanzi was spending incredible hours of his awake time operating on people from a 'distant land', she also told him that she had heard of his advocacy for women. If his grandmother had talked in the tone she used on her grandson, to a different person, it was sure to offend them, but for Maanzi, it was a wakeup call, a resolution made, and a passion sealed, his desire to do medicine had started with his aunt, and now she had died of a pregnancy complication. From that day on, Maanzi decided, that he would talk about maternal deaths, to everyone and anyone who dared to listen. He decided that he would go back to medical school and specialize in obstetrics and gynecology.

As Maanzi went back and immersed himself into his work, every day, he could not help but reflect deeply on how the lack of education, perhaps had contributed to his aunt's demise, since she did not have many options for private health care. Or maybe it was just the poor healthcare infrastructure. He also thought often of Kesi and enquired about her when he called his parents.

Chapter 24

IN THE MEANTIME, KESI'S WORLD HAD COME COLLAPSING ON HER head.

She was at her grandparents' home being told to return to her prodigal father, but she would not have any of it. She was pleading to be allowed to go see her mother, maybe, she alone would have a solution for her daughter.

"My mother will have a solution to this madness," she thought to herself.

She did not know her mother well, because she had not really grown up with her, but this was the only person she could now turn to. So, she left her grandparents' house and went to visit Zuri, whom she had not seen in about four years.

Their first meeting was traumatic to both women. Kesi was not impressed with what she saw her mother had become.

"Mum, how can you allow yourself to be treated like this?" she asked.

She was so furious when she saw all the scars on her mother's once-beautiful face. The scars were, old, healing and some fresh.

Maybe it was the distance. But she was very detached from her mother and did not hold any of her opinions back. One never talked to their parents like that in this part of the world. But Kesi had fought to get herself out of a difficult situation and did not understand why her mother remained helpless.

"Why don't you leave him?" she asked.

"Stop it. I say, stop that nonsense," Zuri snapped. "You do not get to talk to me like that; you have not lived long enough to see how the world works." Then, realizing her anger would not help, she said, "I can't leave." "I have small children here who need me," Zuri responded.

After that, she pulled her daughter in an embrace and held her close for a long while.

"How have you been, my little girl, my hope?"

In her shock, Kesi had blurted out the first thing that came to her mind and forgot all the usual pleasantries that people greeted each other with.

"Have you been safe and well with Uncle Jude?" Zuri asked.

"I have not been living with your Uncle Jude for a while," Kesi replied to her mother's horror. Zuri quickly let her go from the embrace, looking straight into her daughter's eye, with that look of 'tell me what has been happening'.

She did not need to ask Kesi to explain.

Kesi told her mother what had been going on in her life since she went to live with Uncle Jude and then her father.

"Whaaaat?

You were living where?

With whom?

For how long?" Zuri could not seem to wrap her mind around what was being said.

"Wait, wait, wait, wait," Zuri was distraught and feeling dizzy. She staggered to the ground and sat on a mat.

"I am so sorry that I was not able to take care of you. I am so sorry that I cannot take care of you, and you cannot stay here either," she said as she buried her head into her palms and wept.

"Mum, it will be okay," Kesi said. "I surely cannot go back to live with my father. I would rather give up school."

Zuri dried her tears, looked at her daughter, and after a long while pointed to her bag.

"Please reach into my bag and get me my mobile phone," she said resolutely.

After Kesi gave Zuri the phone, she scrolled through her phone book, dialled a number, and then waited as she heard the phone begin to ring.

Ring, ring, ring, silence was palpable between the two. Then Kesi broke the silence.

"Who are you calling?" Kesi asked.

"Uncle Maanzi," she replied.

"Yeah, another uncle of mine," teased Kesi.

"He is your real uncle. He made me a promise, and I know he will make good of it. Now is the time to remind him."

Gesturing to Kesi to keep quiet, Zuri began her conversation.

"Doctor, this is Zuri," she said.

"Oh, Zuri, how are you?" Maanzi replied, glad she had called. "How have you been?"

But Zuri was not wasting any time. "Do you remember when I asked you to take care of my daughter for me?"

Maanzi was just leaving the hospital gate, heading to his small one-bedroom house that this missionary hospital provided for accommodation within its compound. With his right hand holding the phone and his left hand on his forehead, he replied, "Of course I remember." He hated this question and hated her asking it. But she had asked him one time too often, and he was ashamed that he did not know where Kesi was at the time. She had asked him, and he had said he would look after her, but he had failed her yet again. Maybe he should have tried to fight the cultural bureaucracy that had denied him the opportunity of taking care of Kesi, and instead favoured Kesi's grandparents and then Great Uncle Jude.

Maybe he should have constantly been nosy and checking to see where she was and what she was doing. Maanzi thought to himself at that moment.

But instead, he had accepted that Kesi's grandparents had greater claim over her, and he didn't want to object if they decided to send her somewhere else. He had also justified that helping his parents to pay school fees for his many siblings was taking up a huge chunk of his resources, and at the moment, he could not afford it. He had thought of blaming his busy schedule for not following up with Kesi, but all the reasons came up short. Zuri had asked him one time too many, and he had failed her each time. They needed to break this cycle before it was too late for Kesi. He thought about his aunt, and the memories were very painful to bear. He could not wait any longer to help Kesi before it was too late, just like with his aunt. He resolved.

"Well, I need your help," Zuri said.

Zuri spoke for a few minutes, but since this was a "fee for service" phone, Maanzi said, "You hang up, and I will call you back shortly. I have quite enough credit on my phone that is paid for."

"Thank you," Zuri said; she hung up and waited for it to ring again.

She was sitting at the edge of her chair, rocking back and forth; her daughter noticed how apprehensive she was and asked, "What happened? Why did you hang up?"

"Are you sick mom, I heard you talk about a Doctor?" Kesi asked her mom, looking concerned.

"I did not hang up, he is going to call me back," she said.

A few minutes later, the phone started to ring, it was Maanzi calling back. With sweaty hands, Zuri pounced on the phone as if it would run away and started to speak again, this time more relaxed. After a while, she stretched out her arm to give the phone over to her daughter.

"Here, Kesi, it's Uncle Maanzi. He would like to speak with you."

With distrusting eyes, Kesi received the phone from her mother and immediately put it to her ear.

"Hello, little Kesi," he began. "My name is Maanzi. Your mother and I grew up together. I would like to help with your school fees."

Silence.

"Hello, hello?" Maanzi was speaking into a silence on the other side of the conversation.

"Hello, I am still here," Kesi responded.

"What do you want to do with your life after school?" Maanzi asked.

"I want to be a teacher," Kesi replied. "I would love to teach children."

There was a long pause as if the phone line had gone dead.

"Hello, hello, Uncle Maanzi, are you still there?" Kesi enquired.

"Yes, I am still here," he replied. "Very good, if you want to become a teacher, I will help you. I want you to study hard, give it all your best, and let me do the worrying about finding school fees."

"Okay," Kesi quietly replied, unwilling to believe that it would be that easy.

She was still suspicious that this Uncle Maanzi would pretend to be good when her mother was around and then turn his back on her when she really needed his help.

"Thank you and bye," she said, keeping it simple as she handed the phone to her mother.

Getting back on the phone, Kesi saw tears in her mother's eyes as she spoke into the phone. Her mum was wiping tears, sneezing, and biting her lips.

"Just like old times, eh," Zuri was speaking into the phone.

"I will take care of your daughter for you. I promise you, this time I will," Maanzi was saying, and Zuri was sobbing, shaking her head, and saying, "Thank you, thank you, thank you."

Putting the phone away, looking straight into her daughter's eyes, Zuri reached out her once smooth hands, now rough from hard labour and physical abuse, and took Kesi's little hands.

"Uncle Maanzi is going to take you to a private boarding school; you can now study and become a teacher, or anything you ever want ... anything. So now that school is settled for you, let's have some food. You must be hungry."

"Mum, tell me about Uncle Maanzi," Kesi said.

"Maanzi is a doctor. It is difficult to believe it sometimes," Zuri said with a grin on her face as if she was thrown back to the old days.

Zuri continued, "Maanzi and I were very good friends. We had been so as soon as we could understand. We played together, dreamed together. In fact, when Uncle Maanzi decided he wanted to be a doctor, I wanted to be a teacher."

"Whaat?" Kesi said. "Really? A teacher no way!"

"I really wanted to be a teacher," said Zuri, "and then one day ..."

"And then what happened one day?" Kesi asked.

"Never mind, you must be starving. Anyhow, since I have not seen you for a long time, tell me about yourself." She changed the topic and instead asked Kesi what her plans would be now that she will have her school fees fully paid for.

They both talked deep into the evening, and soon it was time for Kesi to go back to her grandparents' home. So, the mother and daughter bid each other good-bye, and Kesi returned home, where she prepared for her new life in a boarding school, a life with a promise of limitless opportunities and hope.

Immediately after he got off the phone with Zuri, Maanzi called his parents. His father picked up the phone.

Maanzi had recently bought a cell phone for his parents, so he could call them anytime. "Hello, Maanzi, thank you for the phone. We are very happy with it, and my friends come here to call their children in the city," Francis said. "And your two aunts are here visiting. They want to speak with you too."

"Oh, I am glad the phone is helping," Maanzi replied.

"Hey, Dad, listen," he continued. "I am going to take care of Kesi and start paying her school fees. All you have to do is look after her during the holidays."

"I have talked with Zuri and she has agreed to this plan. I made her a promise and I want to make good of it," Maanzi said.

His parents considered Kesi as their grandchild anyway, so this was not to be a problem. However, Kesi was a problem child in the community since she talked back to her elders. The girl had no filter and many times was considered rude. Maanzi's father had once described her.

"She is very rude, unhelpful, disrespectful. She does not even help with any home chores at her grandparents' house. I think that is why everyone is pushing her away," Francis continued to express his concerns. In any case, you are already stretched for money paying for your siblings.

His father put his wife on the phone, and she also had a few words to describe the 'little girl that did not inspire confidence'.

"But my son, I think you have made up your mind and everyone deserves a second chance, so we will take care of her," Maanzi's mother responded.

Maanzi listened to his parents patiently and then told them that he was well aware of all this. And he tried to ease the tension and sell the little girl to them.

"Just imagine what this poor girl has been through," he said, "moving from home to home, never knowing her father, only to find him and them be mistreated by his wife. She has not known any love and has no love to give; she has been taken advantage of by those she loved, and now she has trust issues. Give her time and a second chance."

"We really hope you are not going to waste money on this girl," Francis said.

"I will take my chances with her, just like you took your chances with me and gave me an opportunity to change my life," Maanzi said.

"Well, we will take care of her for you," Francis responded.

In school, Kesi was so determined to succeed that all she did was study. She had no time to play. She kept to herself most times and read every book she got her hands on. The librarians were her close friends, as she would even come in over the weekends to read or do her homework. After the first term at school, her grades were good, competing favourably with other students who had been in the school for the past year.

During Kesi's first holiday from secondary school, she went again to visit Zuri and her children. Kesi looked very beautiful; she had her mother's eyes and long dark hair, pulled back in a small ponytail. They talked about school and the opportunities that were beginning to open for her.

"I should take a look at that hair before you leave today," Zuri offered.

As she washed her daughter's hair, she told her, "I am really proud of you; you will make a great teacher."

"Thanks, Mum," Kesi replied. "And don't you worry; when I'm done, I will take care of you and my younger brothers and sisters."

Finally, the light was beginning to shine over her world, and Zuri was hopeful. It had been a long time coming, but she could begin to feel the sun's gentle rays begin to pierce her skin. They made their way through the heavy clouds that hung over her head for such a long time. It was probably too late for her now, but she would ensure that it wasn't too late for her children. Never for them. She would make sure of it.

Epilogue

MAANZI CONTINUED TO WORK AS A DOCTOR AND AN ADVOCATE for women's rights and completed a master's degree in Obstetrics and Gynecology. He continued to gravitate to those women who had been marginalized and were victims of a culture that favoured men. He continued to advocate for the rights of girls and women.

His siblings all completed school. This was a first in their village, to have a whole family educated beyond primary school. His siblings have certificates, diplomas and degrees.

One of Maanzi's siblings pursued a political career, hoping to bring real change in their little village. In fact, this brother had an opportunity to compete with the professor who had difficulty giving Maanzi a letter of reference to attend the 'better high school', claiming that there was no reason to help him with the letter since his parents were very poor to afford school fees. Maanzi was quite energized by what his parents and siblings have been able to do. His father, who was once ridiculed by his fellow men in their village, was now respected. He had produced among his children, a doctor and a young politician.

"Imagine the power of education," Maanzi thought to himself.

Zuri worked hard to ensure that her other children went to school. They were still in primary school but were doing well; Kesi was on her way through college to become a teacher. It had not been an easy road, but Maanzi was Hopeful that her life will never be the same because of education.

Maanzi's parents were still not the richest in the village, but they were well respected, and for Maanzi, that was enough. Their children had been given a good start in life, and where they went from there was up to them. As their children, one by one, became independent and started to move away from home, Maanzi's parents started to realize that their sacrifices were indeed beyond them, they were nurturing children for the world and not just their village. Their children wanted to change their world, and their little village was too small for them. But these were good problems to have.

Maanzi spread his wings far beyond his parents' imagination. He ended up moving to Canada to do more medical training where he now lives. He continues to be passionate about maternal and child health and practices obstetrics and gynecology. He also loves to teach and considers himself a lifelong student.

One of Maanzi's happiest moments in life was when his parents made a trip from their remote village to the airport in Uganda for the very first time in their lives, saw their first airplane, boarded that airplane and came to visit him in Canada in the year 2016.

When Maanzi, together with his son of nine months picked them from the airport, he greeted them with, "You are welcome, we made it." He hugged them, and tears rolling down on all their faces, recalling the times when all of them thought, they would not be able to make it for another term in school. The conversations they had during their visit with their son, could make pages of another book.

"The sacrifices were worth it, who would have thought that I would ever be in a plane or come across the world to Canada," his father said during one of the nights they sat reflecting on their journey.

"All we ever wanted for you, was to be able to read and write. To have something that we never had. But I could never have imagined that you would become a doctor and be living in Canada. I would do the things we did over again," his mother also interrupted.

Uncle Jay continued to study; he later earned a college teaching diploma and then a bachelor's degree in education. He now works as a primary school headteacher. He continues to inspire young people to reach for higher goals.

Education helps to unlock everyone's potential, for those who have access to education should never take it for granted, instead, they should use the opportunity to become the best they can be. Maanzi tells anyone who asks about education.